Divided We Fall

T. M. Tritchler

Published by T. M. Tritchler, 2024.

DIVIDED WE FALL

First edition. August 31, 2024.

Copyright © 2024 T. M. Tritchler.

ISBN: 979-8227265548

Written by T. M. Tritchler.

Table of Contents

Divided We Stand: How Government Secrets and Media Warfare Fuel America's Deepening Polarization

By T. M Tritchler

A Brief History

COINTELPRO (short for "Counterintelligence Program") was a series of covert, and often illegal activities conducted by the Federal Bureau of Investigation (FBI) in the United States from the 1950s through the early 1970s. Supposedly the program is no longer in operation, however, it seems obvious to this researcher that the tactics are still very much alive and well, and in use by the FBI. The program's main purpose was to surveil, infiltrate, disrupt, and discredit various civil rights organizations, activist groups, politicians, and individuals deemed to be subversive or posing a threat to the government's interests.

The COINTELPRO operations were initially justified as efforts to protect national security and prevent the spread of communism. However, the program often went beyond lawful boundaries and violated individuals' civil rights, leading to criticism and legal challenges. The program's activities were exposed when The Citizens' Commission to Investigate the FBI was an activist group operational in the US during the early 1970ss broke into an FBI office in Media, Pennsylvania, in 1971 and obtained documents detailing COINTELPRO's operations. They stole over one thousand documents and mailed them to news outlets to include television and newspapers. The Washington Post, after establishing the authenticity of the files which the Commission sent them, ran a front-page story on March 24, 1971.

Following these revelations and growing public concern, COINTELPRO was officially terminated in 1971. The program's revelations led to the government assuring the public that increased oversight of intelligence agencies would happen and contributed to the passage of laws aimed at protecting civil liberties. The Author acknowledges that the stated intent is in keeping with the rights of the citizens of our country, however, maintains that the blunder has only served to further purposes of gaining more control over the citizens of our country through political, economic, and social engineering means. The success of the program and subsequent disclosure of the program to the public has in no way dissuaded government officials or those that work in our alphabet agencies from continuing use of the tactics outlined by the COINTELPRO program.

I the author aim to not only educate about this domestic operation against the sovereign citizens of the United States, but to also make the case that this operation never ceased and is in fact still going on today. It is the duty and right of every citizen to bring to light information so that justice may be served.

I would like to acknowledge that the original members of the Citizens' Commission to Investigate the FBI in their bravery exposed a hard truth about the underhandedness of our government, and the lengths to which they will go. A much deserved (in my not so humble opinion) historical marker now sits at the sight of the greatest break-in and theft that most have never heard of.

How We Know About COINTELPRO

Declassified Documents: Many of the details about COINTELPRO became known through declassified FBI documents, released under the Freedom of Information Act (FOIA). These documents included internal memos, reports, and directives that outlined the strategies and goals of COINTELPRO.

Activist Lawsuits: Lawsuits filed by targeted groups and individuals led to the release of additional documents and further exposed the FBI's tactics. The most famous of these is the 1971 break-in at an FBI office in Media, Pennsylvania, by a group of activists who uncovered COINTELPRO files, leading to public outrage.

Congressional Hearings: The Church Committee hearings in the mid-1970s provided a comprehensive investigation into COINTELPRO and other intelligence abuses, offering a detailed public account of the program's activities.

A SCOPE of TACTICS

COINTELPRO targeted a wide range of groups and individuals, including civil rights activists, anti-war protestors, communist and socialist organizations, Black Panther Party members, feminist groups, Native American activists, and more. Upon reading, it appears as if these same tactics are currently in use against parents' groups, militia groups, conservatives, faith-based organizations, and even our former President, as well as other grassroots organizations dedicated to animal rights, climate initiatives, and several religious and cultural groups.

Despite the claim of official termination of the program, this researcher believes that the program is still, in effect, gaslighting the American public thereby undermining freedom, liberty and the pursuit of happiness. COINTELPRO appears to be ongoing under a new operational name, though admittedly the new name is unclear at this time. The program once acknowledged by the FBI involved tactics to include but not limited to such as:

Surveillance and Wiretapping: The FBI monitored targeted individuals and groups through extensive surveillance, including wiretapping phones, intercepting mail, and bugging meetings and private spaces.

Infiltration: Agents and informants were embedded in targeted organizations, often assuming leadership roles to gather intelligence, provoke internal conflicts, and influence the group's activities. These infiltrators would sometimes incite radical actions or confrontations to create discord.

False Flag Operations: The FBI orchestrated activities to appear as though they were conducted by the targeted groups, aiming to portray them as violent or dangerous.

Provocateurs: Agents and informants deliberately provoked confrontations or illegal actions within the groups to foster internal turmoil and division.

Spread of Disinformation: The FBI disseminated false information and rumors to create confusion and distrust within targeted groups, weakening their cohesion and effectiveness.

Forged Documents: The FBI produced and distributed counterfeit documents to tarnish the reputations of activists and organizations.

Harassment: Targeted individuals and groups faced various forms of harassment, including surveillance, frequent law enforcement interviews, intimidation, and legal actions.

Extortion and Threats: The FBI used threats of revealing sensitive information or criminal history to coerce individuals into cooperating.

Media Manipulation: The FBI influenced media outlets to publish negative stories or promote narratives that discredited activists and groups.

Divide and Conquer: Agents fostered internal divisions within organizations by exacerbating existing tensions and causing disagreements over tactics and goals.

Sabotage of Activities: The FBI disrupted events, meetings, and protests by spreading misinformation or using other tactics to undermine group activities.

Legal Actions: The FBI employed legal measures such as false arrests or tax audits to harass and disrupt targeted individuals and groups.

Discrediting Leaders: COINTELPRO aimed to undermine influential leaders by spreading false information about their personal lives, affiliations, or intentions to diminish their credibility.

Creating Dissension: Agents exploited internal conflicts within organizations, spreading rumors or fabricated stories to foster suspicion and infighting.

Fabricating Evidence: The FBI created false documents to make it appear as if targeted groups participated in illegal or violent activities, damaging their image.

Anonymous Threats: Agents sent anonymous threats to instill fear and disrupt activities among activists and groups.

Sabotaging Communications: The FBI tampered with mail and telephone communications, causing confusion and frustration among group members.

Selective Prosecution: Activists were selectively prosecuted for minor offenses unrelated to their political activities to disrupt their involvement in social causes.

Harassment of Supporters: Individuals and businesses supporting targeted groups also faced harassment, surveillance, or legal actions.

Creating Internal Documents: The FBI fabricated internal documents to make it seem like targeted groups were advocating illegal or violent actions.

Psychological Warfare: The FBI used threats, false information, and manipulation to create uncertainty, distrust, and paranoia within targeted organizations.

Preventing Coalition Building: The FBI spread rumors to prevent collaboration between different activist groups, creating distrust and division.

Creating False Confessions: Individuals were coerced or tricked into making false confessions to incriminate themselves or their associates.

Manipulating Legal Proceedings: The FBI influenced legal proceedings by providing false evidence or testimony, leading to unjust prosecutions and convictions.

Media Blackouts: The FBI pressured media outlets to avoid covering certain events or issues related to targeted groups, limiting the spread of their messages.

Harassment of Family Members: The families of activists were targeted with surveillance and harassment to create personal distress and pressure activists to cease their activities.

Use of Informants' Testimony: The FBI relied on the testimony of informants to provide exaggerated or false claims about targeted groups' intentions and actions.

Covert Funding: The FBI secretly funded individuals or groups aligned with its objectives to manipulate their activities or gather intelligence.

Covert Psychological Operations (PSYOPS): Psychological tactics were employed to manipulate perceptions and actions, such as spreading false rumors and using psychological pressure to create paranoia.

Interference with Legal Counsel: The FBI attempted to compromise the attorney-client relationship by surveilling or harassing legal representatives of targeted individuals or groups.

Creating False Front Organizations: The FBI established fake organizations to disseminate propaganda and false information to both activists and the public.

Creating Fake Demonstrations: False demonstrations or events were organized to mislead activists or disrupt their plans.

Use of Coercion and Extortion: Coercion and extortion were used to force individuals to cooperate or provide information.

Use of Psychological Profiles: Psychological profiles were developed to predict behavior and actions of activists, facilitating more effective manipulation.

Infiltration of Leadership: Agents infiltrated the leadership of targeted organizations to influence their decisions and actions, causing ideological splits and conflicts.

Use of Psychological Warfare Experts: Experts in psychological warfare were employed to exploit the psychological vulnerabilities of activists and groups, manipulating emotions, and creating mistrust.

Suppression of Publications: The FBI pressured publishers and distributors to suppress materials from targeted groups, limiting their ability to spread their messages.

Infiltration of Legal Defense Teams: Legal defense teams of targeted individuals were infiltrated to compromise legal strategies and confidential information.

Disruption of Fundraising: Fundraising efforts were interfered with by spreading rumors about financial mismanagement to deter potential donors.

Use of False Identities: False identities were used to interact with activists and groups, obscuring true motives and affiliations.

Manipulation of Public Perceptions: The FBI manipulated public opinion by leaking selective information to portray targeted groups negatively or as threats to national security.

Creation of Dossiers: Detailed dossiers on activists and organizations were compiled, including personal and political information, to use for coercion or extortion.

Exploitation of Personal Relationships: Personal relationships within targeted groups were exploited to amplify tensions and disrupt cohesion.

Forced Relocations: Pressure was applied to force individuals to relocate, disrupting their involvement in activism.

Intimidation and Psychological Pressure: Tactics such as late-night calls, anonymous threats, and surveillance created an atmosphere of fear and intimidation.

Sabotage of Personal Relationships: False rumors were spread to strain personal relationships and erode support networks.

Discrediting Whistleblowers: Individuals who exposed COINTELPRO operations were discredited or subjected to character assassination to undermine their credibility.

HISTORICAL TARGETS

The FBI's COINTELPRO (Counterintelligence Program) targeted a wide range of individuals, organizations, and movements primarily in the 1950s through the 1970s according to the FBI, though as stated earlier by all accounts it is ongoing. The primary targets from the 1950's through the 1970's included:

Civil Rights Movement Leaders

Martin Luther King Jr.: Targeted due to his leadership in the Civil Rights Movement and his calls for racial equality and social justice. The FBI sought to discredit him and his movement through various forms of harassment and surveillance. The FBI's attempts to discredit Martin Luther King Jr. were extensive, part of a broader campaign under the COINTELPRO (Counterintelligence Program) initiative. Here's a detailed account of the tactics used on Dr. King.

Surveillance and Wiretapping

Authorization and Implementation: In 1963, FBI Director J. Edgar Hoover received authorization from Attorney General Robert F. Kennedy to wiretap King's phones and place him under surveillance. The justification was the FBI's belief that King had communist ties, specifically through his association with Stanley Levison, a former advisor with alleged communist connections.

Content and Use of Surveillance: The FBI recorded King's private conversations, particularly those involving sexual affairs, with the intent of using this information against him. Agents monitored King's activities and reported back on any potentially scandalous behavior.

Blackmail Attempt: The Infamous "Suicide Letter": In November 1964, the FBI sent an anonymous letter to King, known as the "suicide letter." The letter, accompanied by a tape containing recordings of King's extramarital activities, was intended to humiliate and pressure him. The letter, written to appear as if it was from a disillusioned supporter, accused King of being a fraud, urged him to kill himself, and threatened to expose his private life publicly if he did not comply.

Psychological Pressure: The letter and tape were timed to arrive just before King was to receive the Nobel Peace Prize, in an effort to induce enough stress and shame to drive him to suicide or at least weaken his public standing.

Disinformation Campaign

Media Manipulation: The FBI fed negative information about King to the press. For example, Hoover publicly labeled King as "the most notorious liar in the country" in 1964. The FBI also planted stories in the media that suggested King was a communist sympathizer, a moral degenerate, and untrustworthy.

Undermining King's Reputation: The FBI worked behind the scenes to undermine King's relationships with political allies and supporters. They spread rumors and fabricated evidence of his supposed communist affiliations and moral shortcomings.

Attempts to Divide King's Support Base: The FBI attempted to create friction between King and other leaders in the civil rights movement. By spreading rumors and misinformation, they hoped to sow discord within the movement and weaken its effectiveness.

Influencing Public Perception: The FBI sought to diminish King's influence by attempting to sway public opinion against him. They did this by leaking damaging information to influential figures and trying to sever his ties with prominent supporters, both black and white.

Undermining International Recognition: When King was nominated for the Nobel Peace Prize, the FBI attempted to dissuade the Nobel Committee from awarding it to him. They sent derogatory reports and dossiers about King to various international contacts, hoping to influence the decision. Despite these efforts, King was awarded the Nobel Peace Prize in 1964.

Strain on Marriage: The FBI's harassment extended to King's personal life. By informing his wife, Coretta Scott King, about his infidelities (gleaned from wiretaps and surveillance), the FBI hoped to cause marital discord. The agency believed that personal turmoil could distract King and weaken his resolve.

Surveillance of Associates: The FBI also targeted King's close associates, hoping to find leverage or create divisions within his inner circle. By tapping the phones and monitoring the movements of King's advisors and friends, the FBI aimed to isolate him and undermine his support network.

Exposure of COINTELPRO: The FBI's campaign against King was part of the larger COINTELPRO operations, which targeted various civil rights leaders, political activists, and organizations. The full extent of these activities became known in the 1970s after the

Church Committee investigations, leading to widespread condemnation and calls for reform of the FBI's practices.

Impact on King's Legacy: Despite the FBI's efforts, King's legacy as a leader of the civil rights movement remained strong. The exposure of the FBI's actions against him further highlighted the injustices he fought against and has led to a more critical understanding of the government's role during that period.

These details illustrate the lengths to which the FBI went to discredit Martin Luther King Jr., using a combination of surveillance, psychological pressure, media manipulation, and attempts to disrupt his personal and professional life.

Black Power and Nationalist Groups:

The Black Panther Party: Known for its militant stance on racial issues and its community programs, the Black Panthers were extensively surveilled and infiltrated.

Malcolm X: Initially targeted as a leader of the Nation of Islam and later as a prominent figure in the broader Black Power movement.

Infiltration by Informants and Undercover Agents

Planting Informants: The FBI recruited individuals to join the Black Panther Party as informants. These informants provided detailed reports on the party's activities, internal communications, and plans. For instance, William O'Neal, an informant who infiltrated the Illinois chapter of the BPP, played a crucial role in providing information that led to the deadly raid on the home of Fred Hampton, a prominent Black Panther leader, in December 1969.

Undercover Agents: FBI agents posed as activists or sympathizers to gain the trust of BPP members. These undercover operatives collected intelligence, sowed discord, and, in some cases, encouraged illegal activities to justify subsequent arrests and raids.

Electronic Surveillance

Wiretapping: The FBI used wiretaps to monitor the phone conversations of key BPP leaders. This allowed the FBI to track the group's plans, alliances, and internal conflicts. Conversations were recorded and used to build cases against members or to anticipate and counteract their activities.

Bugging and Physical Surveillance: In addition to wiretaps, the FBI placed listening devices in homes, offices, and vehicles of BPP members. Agents also conducted physical surveillance, following members, and observing their interactions and movements.

Psychological Warfare

Disinformation Campaigns: The FBI spread false information within the BPP to create mistrust and paranoia among members. For example, they would send anonymous letters or fabricate documents suggesting that certain members were cooperating with the police or were planning to take over the leadership. This tactic fueled internal conflicts and weakened the organization from within.

Fake Letters: The FBI sent fake letters between members or from alleged sympathizers to incite suspicion and create rifts. These letters often contained fabricated accusations of betrayal or plans for mutiny within the party.

Media Manipulation: The FBI fed negative stories to the press to tarnish the BPP's public image. They exaggerated or fabricated reports of violence, criminal activity, and communist affiliations to sway public opinion against the Panthers.

Legal and Harassment Tactics

Targeted Arrests: The FBI worked with local law enforcement to target BPP members for arrest on minor charges, using these arrests to disrupt operations and deplete resources. The frequent legal battles drained the organization financially and mentally.

"Hard" Arrests and Raids: In many cases, arrests were conducted violently, and raids on BPP offices often involved excessive force. These tactics aimed to intimidate members and reduce their capacity to organize. The raid on Fred Hampton's apartment, which resulted in his assassination, is one of the most notorious examples of this approach.

Tax Evasion and Legal Prosecution: The FBI encouraged local authorities to pursue legal action against BPP members on charges such as tax evasion or weapons violations. These prosecutions were intended to disrupt leadership and create a climate of fear within the organization.

Creating Internal Conflicts

Exacerbating Factionalism: The FBI exploited existing tensions within the BPP by promoting factionalism. They would pit members against each other by spreading rumors or by manipulating relationships with other activist groups. For instance, they sought to create conflicts between the Panthers and other Black nationalist groups, like the United Slaves (US Organization), leading to violent confrontations.

Encouraging Extremist Behavior: In some cases, informants or undercover agents encouraged more radical and illegal actions, which would then be used to justify a crackdown on the BPP. This not only increased the group's vulnerability to law enforcement actions but also damaged its public image.

Surveillance of Allies and Supporters

Monitoring Support Networks: The FBI did not just target the Panthers; they also surveilled and harassed their allies and supporters, including lawyers, journalists, and other activists. By weakening the BPP's broader support network, the FBI aimed to isolate the group and reduce its effectiveness.

Disrupting Funding and Resources: The FBI pressured businesses and individuals who supported the Panthers financially, cutting off critical resources. They also infiltrated or disrupted fundraising efforts, making it harder for the BPP to sustain its operations.

Media Smear Campaigns

Character Assassination: The FBI systematically spread disinformation to portray the BPP as a violent, criminal organization.

They labeled the group as a threat to public safety and national security, which influenced public perception and justified aggressive law enforcement actions.

Public Relations Sabotage: The FBI sought to undermine the BPP's community programs, like the Free Breakfast for Children Program, by spreading rumors that the food was contaminated or by intimidating local businesses that supported these initiatives.

Coordination with Local Law Enforcement

Joint Task Forces: The FBI often collaborated with local police departments, sharing intelligence, and coordinating actions against the Panthers. These joint efforts included raids, arrests, and surveillance, ensuring that the BPP was constantly under pressure from multiple angles.

Training and Resources: The FBI provided training and resources to local law enforcement to better equip them to deal with the Panthers. This included sharing surveillance technology, tactical training for raids, and legal support for prosecutions.

Outcome

Dismantling the BPP: The FBI's multi-faceted approach of surveillance, infiltration, harassment, and propaganda eventually succeeded in weakening the Black Panther Party. Internal divisions, financial strain, and constant legal battles led to a significant decline in the organization's influence and membership by the mid-1970s.

The FBI's campaign against the Black Panthers is a stark example of how government agencies can use a combination of covert operations, legal maneuvers, and psychological tactics to undermine political organizations they perceive as threats. The BPP's legacy, however, continues to be a powerful symbol of resistance and community activism.

Anti-Vietnam War Activists:

Students for a Democratic Society (SDS): A leading anti-war organization that was subject to infiltration and disruption by the FBI.

The Weather Underground: A radical leftist group that emerged from SDS, involved in militant actions against the Vietnam War and U.S. imperialism.

Communist and Socialist Organizations:

Communist Party USA: Monitored due to its association with Marxist ideology and perceived threat to national security.

Socialist Workers Party: Targeted for its radical political stance and opposition to U.S. government policies.

Women's Rights Activists:

National Organization for Women (NOW): Targeted due to its advocacy for gender equality and women's rights. The National Organization for Women (NOW), founded in 1966, was targeted by the FBI and other governmental entities largely due to its advocacy for gender equality and women's rights, which were seen as potentially disruptive to the status quo. While NOW was not targeted as aggressively as groups like the Black Panther Party or civil rights organizations, it still faced significant surveillance and attempts to undermine its influence. Here's how NOW was targeted:

Surveillance and Monitoring

FBI Surveillance: The FBI conducted surveillance on NOW, particularly during the height of the feminist movement in the late 1960s and 1970s. This involved monitoring the activities of key leaders, tracking the organization's meetings, and gathering intelligence on its strategies and alliances.

COINTELPRO Operations: While COINTELPRO primarily focused on more radical groups, feminist organizations like NOW were occasionally included in broader surveillance efforts due to their advocacy for social change. The FBI collected information on NOW's activities, though the intensity of this surveillance was less than that of groups deemed more radical or militant.

Infiltration

Use of Informants: The FBI placed informants within feminist organizations, including NOW, to report on their activities and internal dynamics. These informants were tasked with identifying key leaders, understanding the organization's strategies, and reporting on potential links to other social movements, particularly those with more radical or leftist agendas.

Disruption of Alliances: The FBI sought to weaken NOW by disrupting its alliances with other social movements, particularly the civil rights and anti-war movements. By monitoring and spreading disinformation, the FBI aimed to create divisions and reduce the effectiveness of these coalitions.

Media Manipulation

NOW

Negative Publicity: The FBI worked to influence media coverage of NOW and the broader feminist movement. By framing feminist demands as radical or un-American, the FBI and other governmental entities sought to discredit the movement in the eyes of the public. This often involved highlighting fringe elements or more extreme rhetoric within the movement to paint a distorted picture of its goals.

Undermining Feminist Leaders: The FBI attempted to discredit feminist leaders associated with NOW by leaking information (true or fabricated) that would damage their reputations. This could include personal details or exaggerated claims about their political affiliations.

Harassment of Members

Intimidation Tactics: Individual members of NOW, particularly those who were outspoken or played significant roles in the organization, sometimes faced harassment. This could include being followed, receiving threatening phone calls, or having their homes and offices subjected to searches.

Legal Pressure: While less common, some NOW leaders faced legal scrutiny or were subjected to investigations, particularly if they participated in broader social justice movements. The threat of legal action or government scrutiny was used to intimidate activists and discourage participation in the movement.

Attempts to Divide the Movement

Exacerbating Internal Conflicts: The FBI sought to exploit and exacerbate internal divisions within NOW and the broader feminist movement. By spreading rumors or encouraging factionalism, the FBI aimed to weaken the movement's unity and effectiveness. This could involve highlighting disagreements over strategy, such as differences between more radical feminists and those advocating for more moderate reforms.

Targeting Diverse Feminist Voices: The FBI was particularly concerned about the intersection of feminism with other social justice causes, such as racial equality and anti-war activism. By targeting leaders who participated in multiple movements, the FBI hoped to prevent the formation of a broad-based coalition that could challenge the status quo on multiple fronts.

Outcome

Impact on Movement: While the FBI's actions against NOW were less intense compared to other organizations, they still contributed to a climate of suspicion and paranoia within the feminist movement. The surveillance and attempts to discredit leaders created additional challenges for an already embattled movement.

Legacy of Resistance: Despite these efforts, NOW continued to grow and played a crucial role in advancing women's rights in the United States. The organization's resilience in the face of government scrutiny is a testament to its strength and the commitment of its members to gender equality.

Native American Activists:

American Indian Movement (AIM): Targeted for its efforts to address Indigenous rights and sovereignty issues. The American Indian Movement (AIM) was targeted by the FBI and other government agencies due to its activism for Indigenous rights, sovereignty, and its efforts to address systemic injustices faced by Native Americans. AIM's strong stance against government policies and its involvement in high-profile protests and occupations made it a primary target of COINTELPRO. Here's how AIM was specifically targeted and how we know about these efforts:

Surveillance and Monitoring

Extensive Surveillance: AIM leaders and members were subjected to constant surveillance by the FBI. This included wiretaps, monitoring of phone conversations, mail interception, and physical surveillance. The FBI tracked AIM's activities closely, gathering intelligence on its leadership, strategies, and alliances.

Dossiers on Leaders: The FBI maintained detailed dossiers on AIM leaders such as Dennis Banks, Russell Means, and Clyde Bellecourt. These files contained information on their personal lives, political activities, and any perceived vulnerabilities that could be exploited.

FBI Memoranda: Internal FBI documents reveal the extent of surveillance on AIM. For example, FBI memoranda from the 1970s discuss strategies for monitoring AIM activities and preventing the group from gaining traction.

Infiltration and Informants

Infiltration by Undercover Agents: The FBI placed undercover agents within AIM to gather intelligence and disrupt the organization from within. These agents attended meetings, reported on internal discussions, and attempted to influence decisions in ways that would weaken AIM.

Use of Informants: The FBI recruited informants from within the Native American community to spy on AIM. These informants provided detailed reports on AIM's activities, leaders, and plans. Some informants were coerced into cooperating with the FBI through threats or promises of leniency in legal matters.

Sabotage of Operations: Infiltrators sometimes engaged in acts of sabotage, such as providing false information to create confusion or encouraging illegal activities to justify subsequent arrests and crackdowns.

COINTELPRO Tactics

Discrediting AIM Leaders: The FBI used COINTELPRO tactics to discredit AIM leaders. This included spreading false rumors about their personal lives, political affiliations, and intentions. For example, the FBI sought to portray AIM leaders as violent extremists or as being influenced by foreign communist powers.

Inciting Conflict: The FBI attempted to incite conflict between AIM and other Native American groups, as well as within AIM itself. This was done by spreading misinformation, creating fake letters, and exploiting existing tensions. The goal was to create distrust and weaken the movement through internal strife.

Media Manipulation: The FBI fed negative stories about AIM to the press, aiming to shape public perception of the movement as dangerous and unpatriotic. This media campaign portrayed AIM as a violent group, which helped justify government crackdowns.

Legal and Extralegal Harassment

Frequent Arrests: AIM members were frequently arrested on charges ranging from minor infractions to serious criminal offenses. These arrests were often based on trumped-up charges or exaggerated allegations. The goal was to disrupt AIM's activities and drain its resources through constant legal battles.

Raids and Intimidation: AIM offices and community centers were raided by law enforcement agencies, often using excessive force.

These raids were intended to intimidate members and disrupt the organization's operations. For example, during the 1973 Wounded Knee occupation, the FBI and U.S. Marshals surrounded AIM activists, leading to a 71-day standoff that resulted in deaths, injuries, and widespread arrests.

Prosecution of Leaders: AIM leaders were targeted with legal actions to remove them from leadership positions and to intimidate others within the movement. These prosecutions were often based on evidence obtained through illegal surveillance or informant testimony.

Suppression of Protests and Occupations

Wounded Knee Incident (1973): One of the most significant confrontations between AIM and the U.S. government occurred during the Wounded Knee occupation. AIM activists occupied the town of Wounded Knee, South Dakota, to protest corruption within the Bureau of Indian Affairs (BIA) and to demand that the U.S. government honor treaties with Native Americans. The FBI and U.S. Marshals laid siege to the town, leading to a violent standoff that lasted 71 days. This event exemplified the government's determination to suppress AIM's activism.

Oglala Shootout (1975): The FBI's intense pressure on AIM led to a deadly confrontation on the Pine Ridge Reservation in 1975, known as the Oglala shootout. Two FBI agents and one AIM member were killed. The aftermath included a controversial investigation and the conviction of AIM member Leonard Peltier, whose trial has been widely criticized for prosecutorial misconduct and dubious evidence.

Documentation and Public Awareness

Church Committee Investigations (1975-1976): The extent of the FBI's surveillance and infiltration of AIM was partially revealed during the Church Committee hearings in the mid-1970s. These Senate hearings exposed COINTELPRO and other illegal activities by U.S. intelligence agencies, including their actions against AIM. The committee's findings included details of how AIM was targeted, the tactics used, and the impact on the movement.

FOIA Requests and Declassified Documents: Many details of the FBI's actions against AIM have been uncovered through Freedom of Information Act (FOIA) requests and the release of declassified documents. These documents provide a comprehensive look at the government's covert operations against AIM, including surveillance records, internal communications, and reports from informants.

Testimonies and Oral Histories: Former AIM members, activists, and others involved in the movement have provided testimonies and oral histories that corroborate the documented evidence of government targeting. These accounts highlight the psychological and physical toll that FBI harassment took on individuals and the movement as a whole.

Outcome and Legacy

Impact on AIM: The FBI's efforts to undermine AIM through surveillance, infiltration, and harassment had a significant impact. The organization was weakened by internal divisions, constant legal battles, and the loss of key leaders. However, AIM's activism raised awareness of Native American rights and laid the groundwork for future movements advocating for Indigenous sovereignty and justice.

Continuing Struggles: Despite the setbacks, AIM's legacy continues in ongoing struggles for Native American rights and sovereignty. The tactics used against AIM serve as a cautionary tale about the lengths to which the government will go to suppress movements that challenge systemic injustice.

The targeting of AIM by the FBI and other government agencies is well-documented through a combination of government reports, declassified documents, and firsthand accounts, revealing a deliberate and sustained effort to neutralize the organization and its leaders.

Puerto Rican Independence Activists:

Young Lords Organization: Focused on Puerto Rican independence and social justice issues, subjected to FBI scrutiny and disruption.

Other Political Dissidents and Activists:

Anti-Fascist and Civil Liberties Groups: Various organizations and individuals opposing authoritarianism or advocating for civil liberties faced FBI harassment and surveillance.

Dissident Intellectuals: Individuals who challenged mainstream political or social views were often surveilled or discredited. Dissident intellectuals who challenged mainstream political or social views and were often targeted by COINTELPRO included:

Noam Chomsky: A prominent linguist and critic of U.S. foreign policy, Chomsky was surveilled due to his outspoken opposition to the Vietnam War and his criticism of American political and economic systems.

Howard Zinn: A historian and activist known for his critical works on American history, such as "A People's History of the United States," Zinn faced scrutiny for his anti-war activism and leftist perspectives.

Ralph Nader: A consumer rights advocate and political activist known for his critiques of corporate power and government corruption, Nader was monitored due to his influential role in progressive politics and advocacy for reform.

Germaine Greer: A feminist author and activist whose works, including "The Female Eunuch," challenged traditional gender roles and norms, leading to surveillance and attempts to undermine her influence.

Eldridge Cleaver: Though more widely known as a member of the Black Panther Party, Cleaver also gained prominence as an intellectual and writer, particularly with his book "Soul on Ice." His revolutionary views and critiques made him a target for surveillance.

Angela Davis: A scholar and activist known for her involvement in the Black Power movement, Davis was also a prominent feminist and

Marxist theorist. Her political activism and academic work made her a target for COINTELPRO.

Stokely Carmichael (Kwame Ture): A leading figure in the Black Power movement and the Student Nonviolent Coordinating Committee (SNCC), Carmichael's radical views and advocacy for black self-determination attracted FBI attention.

Daniel Berrigan: A Catholic priest and anti-war activist known for his opposition to the Vietnam War and involvement in the Catholic Left, Berrigan was targeted due to his radical religious and political activism.

Herbert Marcuse: A philosopher and sociologist associated with the Frankfurt School, Marcuse's critiques of capitalist society and his influence on student movements made him a target for surveillance.

James Baldwin: A writer and social critic known for his essays and novels addressing race, sexuality, and identity, Baldwin faced surveillance and efforts to discredit him due to his outspoken critiques of racial injustice and American society.

In the U.S., political opponents of authoritarian tendencies or those critical of government policies have faced various forms of surveillance, harassment, and legal challenges.

Targets of COINTELPRO Tactics Since 2000

To make an informed argument that the FBI is still engaged in targeting individuals, groups, and organizations, please take the following information as evidence. Simply put, it is easy to make the case when the tactics listed above are considered.

Critics of the Trump Administration:

Michael Cohen: Former personal attorney to Donald Trump, Cohen faced intense legal scrutiny and harassment after cooperating with investigations into Trump's activities. His imprisonment and public treatment were seen by some as politically motivated retaliation.

Steve Bannon: Former White House Chief Strategist, Bannon faced multiple legal challenges and investigations related to his activities, including charges of fraud. Some perceived these actions as politically motivated efforts to discredit him.

Whistleblowers and Critics of Government Practices:

Chelsea Manning: Manning, who leaked classified information to WikiLeaks, faced extensive surveillance, legal battles, and harsh treatment while imprisoned. Her case has been a prominent example of government attempts to suppress whistleblowing and dissent.

Reality Winner: A former NSA contractor who leaked a classified report on Russian interference in the 2016 election, Winner faced significant legal consequences and public scrutiny, reflecting government efforts to stifle critical information.

Political Activists and Protest Leaders:

Derrick Johnson: President of the NAACP, Johnson has been involved in high-profile civil rights advocacy and has reported instances of surveillance and harassment. The NAACP has historically been a target of surveillance and disruption efforts.

Patrisse Cullors: Co-founder of the Black Lives Matter movement, Cullors has faced scrutiny, harassment, and attempts to discredit her work, especially during high-profile moments of activism.

Journalists Investigating Sensitive Topics:

Aaron Maté: A journalist known for his reporting on issues related to the Russia investigation and anti-war advocacy, Maté has faced attempts to discredit his reporting and questions about his political biases.

Sharyl Attkisson: A former CBS journalist who reported on government surveillance and other sensitive topics, Attkisson has alleged that she was targeted with hacking and surveillance in retaliation for her reporting.

Tucker Carlson has made claims that he was targeted or surveilled by government agencies, particularly the National Security Agency (NSA). In June 2021, Carlson alleged that the NSA was monitoring his communications in an attempt to take his show off the air. It is important to note the NSA responded with a rare public statement, denying that they were monitoring Carlson's communications and asserting that he was not an intelligence target.

Members of Progressive Movements:

Jeremy Scahill: A journalist and co-founder of The Intercept, Scahill has faced harassment and legal challenges related to his investigative journalism on government and corporate misconduct.

Naomi Klein: An author and activist known for her critiques of corporate power and government policies, Klein has been subject to various forms of harassment and attempts to undermine her influence.

Daniel Hale: Whistleblower: Hale, a former U.S. Air Force intelligence analyst, leaked classified information about drone warfare to the media, revealing the civilian casualties caused by drone strikes. He was subsequently charged under the Espionage Act and faced severe legal consequences. His case highlights modern attempts to suppress whistleblowing.

Randy Credico: Political Activist and Comedian: Credico, who engaged in political activism and served as a witness in the Robert Mueller investigation, faced intense scrutiny and harassment, including threats and surveillance, related to his involvement in the investigation and his outspoken views.

Gina Haspel: CIA Director: While Haspel herself is not a direct target, critics and journalists who have investigated her role in the CIA's torture programs or her career have faced significant pushback. The intimidation and legal challenges faced by these critics reflect ongoing attempts to silence dissent regarding controversial figures.

Sarah Kendzior: Journalist and Author: Kendzior, a journalist and author known for her critical reporting on authoritarianism and corruption, particularly related to the Trump administration, has faced targeted harassment, including online threats and attempts to undermine her credibility.

Medea Benjamin: Co-founder of Code Pink: Benjamin, an activist and outspoken critic of U.S. foreign policy and military interventions, has experienced surveillance and harassment. Her activism has led to confrontations with government and corporate interests.

David Cay Johnston: Journalist: Johnston, a journalist known for his investigative work on tax issues and Trump's financial dealings, has faced attempts to discredit his reporting and legal threats related to his work exposing financial corruption.

Glenn Greenwald: Journalist and Author: Greenwald, who has reported extensively on government surveillance and political corruption, continues to face legal and public attacks aimed at discrediting his work and influencing public perception.

Aimee Allison: Founder of She the People: Allison, an activist and founder of She the People, an organization focused on elevating women of color in politics, has faced targeted harassment and attempts to discredit her efforts and activism.

Standing Rock Sioux Tribe: Activists opposing the Dakota Access Pipeline faced significant surveillance and harassment. Reports emerged of law enforcement using private security firms and surveillance technologies to monitor and disrupt the protests.

Disinformation Campaigns:

Russian Disinformation Operations: The 2016 U.S. presidential election saw widespread disinformation campaigns attributed to Russian operatives. These campaigns aimed to influence public opinion and create divisions within American society, paralleling COINTELPRO's disinformation tactics.

COVID-19 Misinformation: During the COVID-19 pandemic, various actors spread misinformation and conspiracy theories, often targeting scientists and health officials, similar to how COINTELPRO spread false information to create confusion and distrust.

Legal and Political Repression:

Political Prosecutions of Activists: High-profile cases like those of activists involved in the Capitol riot on January 6, 2021, or anti-abortion activists who have faced legal challenges reflect contemporary use of legal measures to suppress political dissent. Some critics argue these prosecutions are used to deter activism and create a chilling effect.

Harassment of Journalists:

Julian Assange: Founder of WikiLeaks, Assange has faced extensive legal battles and political persecution, including efforts to extradite him to the U.S. on charges related to the publication of classified documents. This has led to accusations of government overreach and attempts to suppress journalistic activities.

Maria Ressa: A journalist in the Philippines who has faced legal harassment and threats for her critical reporting on the Duterte administration. Her situation highlights the use of legal and extralegal tactics to stifle press freedom.

Surveillance of Online Activities:

NSA Surveillance: The National Security Agency's extensive data collection programs, revealed by Edward Snowden, exemplify modern surveillance practices. Critics argue that these programs infringe on privacy rights and are used to monitor political activists and critics.

Social Media Monitoring: Governments and private companies have been involved in monitoring social media activities of activists and political figures. This includes the collection of personal data and tracking of online behaviors.

Targeted Online Harassment:

Gamergate Controversy: A campaign of online harassment against women and minorities in the gaming industry reflected tactics of intimidation and attempts to suppress dissenting voices. This harassment involved coordinated online attacks and threats designed to create fear and silence critics.

Exposing Whistleblowers and Critics:

Edward Snowden and Chelsea Manning: Both individuals faced intense scrutiny, legal challenges, and public attempts to discredit them after revealing classified information about government surveillance and military actions.

These examples reflect how individuals in the U.S. who challenge government policies or authoritarian tendencies may encounter tactics aimed at surveillance, discrediting, or legal harassment.

COINTELPRO's activities were part of a broader effort to suppress political dissent, and radical movements perceived as threats to U.S. national security and stability. In summary, COINTELPRO, the covert FBI program operational from the late 1950s to the early 1970s, was a critical component of a broader strategy to suppress political dissent and manage radical movements perceived as threats to U.S. national security and stability. Under the leadership of J. Edgar Hoover, COINTELPRO targeted influential civil rights leaders, radical organizations, and anti-war activists using tactics such as surveillance, infiltration, discrediting, and legal harassment. This aggressive effort aimed to neutralize movements that were seen as challenging the existing power structures and political system, reflecting a deep-seated concern over potential instability and threats to national security.

The legacy of COINTELPRO is evident in contemporary efforts to control dissent, revealing a persistent pattern of governmental measures aimed at suppressing perceived threats. Modern surveillance programs, the infiltration of social justice movements, and coordinated media smear campaigns echo the tactics of COINTELPRO, albeit adapted to new technological and political contexts. These parallels underscore the ongoing challenge of balancing national security with the protection of civil liberties, highlighting the need for vigilance in safeguarding democratic processes and ensuring that dissenting voices are not unjustly targeted.

Dr Kilde and other Insiders.

Insiders to COINTELPRO are numerous. Here, however, are the highlights and the basic roles played by key members of the government and the FBI.

COINTELPRO (Counterintelligence Program) was a covert and often illegal FBI operation aimed at surveilling, infiltrating, discrediting, and disrupting domestic political organizations considered subversive or radical. COINTELPRO employed a variety of illegal tactics designed to disrupt, discredit, and neutralize political organizations and individuals deemed threats to national security. Among these tactics were unauthorized wiretaps and covert surveillance, which included intercepting private communications and monitoring activities without legal warrants. The program also involved the infiltration of targeted groups through undercover agents and informants who provided inside information and often engaged in or encouraged illegal activities to discredit the organizations.

Disinformation and smear campaigns were key components of COINTELPRO's strategy. The FBI spread false or misleading information to damage the reputations of individuals and groups, often manipulating media outlets to publish negative and sensationalized stories. Harassment and intimidation were used to deter activism, including threats of violence and disruptive tactics to create confusion and fear. Additionally, illegal raids on offices and homes were conducted without warrants, sometimes resulting in the planting of evidence to frame individuals for crimes they did not commit.

Political and legal manipulation also featured prominently in COINTELPRO's operations. This included entrapment, where individuals were coerced into committing illegal acts that could then be used against them, and selective legal persecution, where laws were enforced in a politically motivated manner to imprison or silence dissenters. These tactics, which violated legal and ethical standards, were integral to COINTELPRO's efforts to suppress political dissent and maintain control over perceived threats to the established order

While the FBI itself, under the direction of J. Edgar Hoover, was the primary agency behind COINTELPRO, several key insiders played significant roles in executing and managing the program:

Edgar Hoover

As the Director of the FBI from 1924 to 1972, Hoover was the architect and chief proponent of COINTELPRO. He was deeply concerned about what he perceived as threats to national security from communist and radical organizations and personally oversaw many of the operations.

Hoover's deep mistrust of civil rights leaders, leftist organizations, and social movements drove the aggressive tactics used in COINTELPRO. His directives often emphasized the need to prevent the rise of leaders who could unify and mobilize marginalized groups.

William C. Sullivan

Sullivan was the head of the FBI's Domestic Intelligence Division during the peak years of COINTELPRO. He was personally responsible for managing the day-to-day operations of the program.

Sullivan oversaw many of the specific campaigns against targeted groups, including the efforts to discredit Martin Luther King Jr. He played a critical role in implementing Hoover's orders and expanding the scope of COINTELPRO.

Sullivan became a critic of some of Hoover's methods later in his career and testified before Congress about the FBI's activities. His later disillusionment with Hoover's leadership added credibility to the revelations about COINTELPRO.

Clyde Tolson

Tolson was the Associate Director of the FBI and Hoover's close confidant. He participated in the overall administration of COINTELPRO and supported Hoover's decisions.

As Hoover's trusted assistant, Tolson was privy to all major FBI operations, including COINTELPRO. His unwavering loyalty to Hoover ensured that the program ran smoothly and without internal opposition.

Cartha "Deke" DeLoach

DeLoach was a high-ranking FBI official and a close associate of Hoover, often described as one of the Director's most trusted aides. He played a significant role in the public relations aspect of COINTELPRO, particularly in managing the FBI's image and dealing with the media.

DeLoach participated in some of the public smear campaigns orchestrated by the FBI, particularly against civil rights leaders like Martin Luther King Jr. He coordinated efforts to leak damaging information to the press and manipulate public opinion.

Roy Mitchell

Mitchell was an FBI agent who played a key role in infiltrating the Black Panther Party (BPP). He was the handler of William O'Neal, an informant who infiltrated the BPP and provided critical information that led to the raid and assassination of Fred Hampton.

Mitchell's management of informants like O'Neal was typical of COINTELPRO's tactics, where the FBI used inside informants to destabilize and neutralize targeted groups from within.

George C. Moore

Moore was an FBI official involved in overseeing surveillance and infiltration operations against Black liberation movements and civil rights organizations. He played a role in coordinating COINTELPRO activities aimed at discrediting and disrupting these groups.

Moore's work was instrumental in the FBI's efforts to divide and weaken movements like the Southern Christian Leadership Conference (SCLC) and the Black Panther Party.

Informants and Undercover Agents

Informants and undercover agents were critical to COINTELPRO's operations. They infiltrated targeted organizations, gathered intelligence, and sometimes engaged in provocative activities to create internal conflicts or provoke illegal actions.

Notable informants included William O'Neal (Black Panther Party), who provided information leading to the raid on Fred Hampton, and Melvin X (Nation of Islam), who spied on the activities of the Nation of Islam.

These informants were instrumental in the FBI's ability to conduct covert actions, leading to the disbandment or significant weakening of several organizations.

Congressional Committees and Investigations

Church Committee: Although not part of COINTELPRO, the Church Committee, led by Senator Frank Church in the 1970s, played a crucial role in exposing the FBI's covert operations. The committee's investigations brought to light the full extent of COINTELPRO's illegal activities.

Pike Committee: Another key investigation was conducted by the Pike Committee, which also revealed details about domestic surveillance programs like COINTELPRO.

These individuals and operations within COINTELPRO worked together to conduct one of the most notorious domestic surveillance programs in U.S. history, targeting a wide array of civil rights, anti-war, and political organizations. The program's legacy continues to influence discussions about government overreach and the protection of civil liberties.

Rauni-Leena Tellervo Luukanen-Kilde née Valve (15 November 1939 – 8 February 2015) was a Finnish physician who wrote and lectured on parapsychology, ufology and mind control. In her book, <u>Bright Light on Black Shadows</u> Dr.Rauni-Leena Luukanen Kilde does not specify where she obtained this instruction manual or who authored it. However, as Chief Medical Officer for Northern Finland, she was an "insider" who was invited to many open and secret conferences. Her husband Sverre Kilde (1987–1996) was also a political insider. Here is a summary of part 1 of the document:

"Harassment Methods: The document outlines various harassment techniques used by organizations like the FBI's COINTELPRO, Operation Gladio, and other covert groups. These methods include surveillance, sabotage, and psychological operations.

Surveillance: Continuous monitoring of targets, including detailed reporting of their daily activities, is emphasized. Both visual and electronic surveillance are used1[1].

Punishment Acts: Agents perform acts to make the target uncomfortable, such as noise disturbances, physical sabotage, and intercepts. These actions are designed to be deniable and make the target appear mentally ill if they complain.

Reputation Sabotage: The document describes strategies to destroy the target's reputation through rumors and discrediting their public statements."

Here is a summary of part 2 of the document:

"Information Warfare: The new war focuses on information warfare, including infrasonic and ultrasonic weapons that can target individuals and cause various physical and psychological effects.

Non-Lethal Weapons (NLW): These weapons are designed to incapacitate without causing permanent injury. They include

---

1.   https://edgeservices.bing.com/edgesvc/

chat?udsframed=1&form=SHORUN&clientscopes=chat,noheader,udsedgeshop,channelstable

,ntpquery,devtoolsapi,udsinwin10,udsdlpconsent,udsfrontload,cspgrd,&shellsig=cac6b8d1a004

0fabd3e88c309fd69f8ce7660d72&setlang=en-

US&lightschemeovr=1&udsps=0&udspp=0#sjevt_0bcef9c45bd8a48eda1b26eb0c61c869_7C

Discover.Chat.SydneyClickPageCitation_0bcef9c45bd8a48eda1b26eb0c61c869_7Cadpclick_

0bcef9c45bd8a48eda1b26eb0c61c869_7C0_0bcef9c45bd8a48eda1b26eb0c61c869_7Ce9aae9

d4-e5e0-44c4-91ff-1042fdf7d59b

biological, chemical, directed-energy weapons, and psychological operations.

Psychological Operations (PsyOp): Aimed at modifying behavior by inflicting pain and demoralizing targets through continuous psychological triggers.

Directed Energy Weapons (DEW): These weapons use concentrated energy to damage or destroy targets, causing a range of physical and psychological effects."

There are clear parallels to the CIA's KUBARK torture manual, which has been employed in Vietnam, Latin America, the Middle East, and in CIA "black sites" and "extraordinary rendition" centers worldwide. The psychological warfare system described here closely mirrors the U.S. military's operations in "Fourth Generation Warfare," "Civil-Military Operations," "Military Operations Other Than War," "Unconventional Warfare," "Asymmetrical Warfare," "Psychological Warfare," and "Information Warfare," as detailed in Rich's New World War: Revolutionary Methods for Political Control. (See Appendices 2 and 3 for a comparison of key terms across these programs.) In fact, these systems are strikingly similar.

The significant revelation is that modern organized gang-stalking operations are virtually identical to those used in the FBI's secret COINTELPRO (Counter-Intelligence Program) of the 1950s-1970s, the clandestine "Gladio" and other "Stay Behind Army" operations in Europe from 1950 to 1990, and the destabilization and citizen-elimination efforts now being conducted globally under the guise of "Counterterrorism" by the U.S. military in approximately 140 of the world's 195 nations (see The World Is the Battlefield: US SOCOM Involved in 134 'Counterterrorism' Wars).

Further details on the advanced technologies currently used in covert global Organized Stalking and Electronic Harassment operations are provided in Appendix 4 (From Total Individual

Control Technology by Omnisense). Dr. Kilde's Chapter 18 is followed by these appendices:

- Appendix 1 : Key words and phrases directly from this manual.

- Appendix 2 : Key terms from Rich's New World War: Revolutionary Methods for Political Control (2011). (ETK comment: The terms, definitions, military documents, laws, and patents provided by Rich confirm the existence of the operations described in Kilde's manual.)

- Appendix 3 : European Parliament Resolution on Operation Gladio.

- Appendix 4 : From Total Individual Control Technology by Omnisense.

1. GENERAL

Operations in general are of the "active surveillance" type. Passive surveillance is

watching a target covertly, to obtain information about the target. Active surveillance can

include information gathering, but it (also) includes the agent making the target aware

They are under surveillance. Beyond active surveillance, agents perform acts to keep the

target uncomfortable, around the clock. Although operations are silently approved of,

and covered for by the official justice system, (they are not) seen as criminal in nature by

citizens who do not have a powerful sense of right and wrong.

Agents must take great care that every act of punishment is DENIABLE. This

means that should the target complain to police, (or) any other officials, or friends,

neighbors, family members, or doctors, the nature of the punishment must be seen as the target's "overactive imagination" or better yet, an indication the target is mentally ill.

(The system) has worked for years to recruit the medical establishment to help maintain

deniability, and today, most targets (are) immediately labeled as mentally ill and often

forced onto anti-psychotic medication when they complain. But their agents must still do

their part skillfully (to) perform acts of punishment, so (that) almost anyone the target

complaints will deny a crime against the target has taken place. As an agent, you will be

trained in how to do this.

(The system) has been blessed with advanced technology which enables heavy

punishment at times the target is in their home, silently, through walls, and this is very

deniable. Agents must pass their initial training and demonstrate an elevated level of

commitment to maintain community safety, and the ability to operate deniably, before

they will be considered for advanced electronic punishment training. Electronic

punishment training is beyond the scope of this manual.

The organization is extremely fortunate in that we have been able to recruit top specialists to

back up field operations people. Psychologists are the key to find(ing) ways to maximize

feelings of stress and hopelessness in the target, and degrading the target's health, from

many individual "minor" invasive punishment acts. Technicians in all fields-

telecommunications, electric power, building electrical and alarm systems, and utility

employees in all fields use their positions to inflict many absolutely "normal looking"

problems on targets on an ongoing basis. And of course, the services of many skilled

locksmiths are invaluable in this. As a community-based agent (CBA) you will have the

privilege of collaborating with a team capable of delivering better "justice" than the official

system.

2. SURVEILLANCE

Surveillance is the foundation of all operations. Both community-based agent (CBA) visual

surveillance and advanced electronic surveillance are used. This chapter will cover only

local agent visual surveillance. Your local lead agent will schedule surveillance watches

for each target in that community. Every target will have at least one CBA watching them

(at) all times, even while at home and asleep. Each CBA surveillance team will be given a

cell phone number for reporting target actions and movement to the local Control Center

(CC).

Actions to be reported include, but are not limited to:

Target turns lights on to start the day.

Target uses toilet or shower

Target exits residence

Target drives away

Target arrives at work, or

Target shops or visits any other establishment or location.

Target arrives home

Target eats meal, at home or in restaurant

Target engages in sexual activity

Target turns lights off at the end of the day

Target turns light on in the middle of the night

Target travels out of town

Some of these observations will be performed by the Electronic Corps (EC), but CBA's

should attempt to make and report as many detailed observations of target activity as

possible. The reason such detail is necessary is that the punishment phase of active

surveillance requires that supervisors customize each punishment action to match the

personality of (the) target, and the need to make each punishment action appear to be

"life's normal breaks."

One important punishment function of surveillance is to sensitize the target. Targets are

never told they are under surveillance or being punished. Instead, close, active

surveillance and other activities, happening far too frequently to be written off as "life's

normal breaks," will eventually cause the target to realize they are under surveillance and

punishment.

As a community-based agent (CBA), you will be given specific instruction(s) on exactly

when, where, and how to conduct punishment actions. If you conduct

punishment instructions exactly as given, there is no way the target will be believed if they complain, and you will not be exposed to risk of action by law enforcement.

How well the punishment actions work depends on how accurate and complete your

reports are in many situations (. The) Control Center (CC) acquires access to properties or

apartments immediately next to the target's homes or apartments. Because EC

(Electronic Corps) has through-the-wall surveillance and punishment equipment, they will

be reporting target activity along with community-based agents. In a typical setup, CBA's

may be posted in a parked car where the target's home or apartment can be observed

overnight, for example.

In this setup, the CBA in the car may be instructed to call, using walkie-talkie-style cell

phones, another CBA (or team) waiting or patrolling by car nearby to follow the target,

or you may be assigned to follow the target yourself. You will receive instructions from

your local center as to following the target.

Targets in transit may be either covertly or visibly followed. When in doubt, hang back a

bit, and contact the center for instructions, as targets in transit can present many

unexpected situations. The Center will always have the target's position monitored, so

if a target gives the CBA the slip, it will assign other appropriate community-based agents

to pick up the target at the earliest opportunity. Be sure to notify (the Control Center) immediately if you lose the target.

When applying the visible following of a target, making the target uncomfortable because

in your presence, you will be given instructions as to when to break off the following.

Another CBA or CBA team may pick up the visible following, but once you have broken

away, they advise that you are clear and ready for the next assignment.

3. INTERCEPTS

Intercepts are where community-based agents (CBA) will appear to "just coincidentally"

cross paths, on foot, with the target. Once the target has been sensitized to the point of

realizing they are under surveillance and punishment, they will recognize, and be made

appropriately uncomfortable by, the simple act of multiple CBA's "just happening to"

cross paths with them.

Your local control center will instruct you as to how you will be cued to perform an

intercept. Often you will have an on-site supervisor (OSS) position you, and give you hand

signals as to when to start your movement to intercept the target. Because targets

moving about are not always predictable, the success of CBA intercepts depends

heavily on the Electronic Corps who have means of monitoring the exact whereabouts of

every target, and through computer programs, predict exactly when and where a target will be as they move about the community. Your local OSS has a special means of

receiving instant, silent instructions for the Center.

1. Intercepting CBAs may be asked to perform one of the following forms of intercept:

2. Simple path crossing, requiring the target to take evasive action to avoid collision,

multiple CBAs sometimes perform this several times during a single outing by a target.

On foot, walking for an extended period on the opposite side of the street from walking

target.

3. Arriving at a place known to be a favorite of the target, and simply occupying that

place just as the target is about to arrive (restaurants, parks, public facility seating, even

bus seats are examples); sometimes just "hanging out" in such a location at times and

places where people do not ordinarily do that.

4. Smoking, coin-jingling, whistling, or toe-tapping near the target at a location where the

target is known to need to stand, as to wait for the bus, or standing right behind a target

at a water fountain.

5. A group, as many as a dozen CBAs, may be assigned to arrive at a store just ahead of a

target, and form a queue ahead of the target, spending time buying lottery tickets, to

delay the target. (The target) is very tired and eager to get home after work, for example,

or in a hurry.

6. Community-based agents may be assigned to leave a next-door home or apartment

the same time as the target, repeatedly. Alternatively, a CBA may intercept the

target a short way before home and arrive at the same time as the target.

While these may seem like trivial acts, keep in mind that the target will have these

"trivial" things happen every single day, and repeated intercepts like these will force the

target to always watch for such acts, ensuring the target never "has a nice

day." This is the goal, to ensure the target's punishment. Similar intercept operations are

performed with vehicles. The Center can schedule these every day the target commutes,

and both to and from work. Vehicle intercepts are particularly effective when the target

sees the same vehicle in an intercept convoy both in the morning and in the evening

commute. (Because vehicle intercepts can be dangerous, CBA assigned to vehicle

intercept duty must successfully complete a special training course prior to actual

assignment.) Here are some examples of vehicle intercepts a community-based agent

(CBA) can expect to be assigned.

-Parking to prevent a target's leaving a parking area, and then disappearing.

-Parking commercial vehicles often, near target's home with something unusual about these vehicles, such as there is no need for that trade, or just unmarked white vans to

make the target think the van is there to conduct surveillance.

-Simple following, or leading, a short distance, but every day. Doing this, both during

target commutes and then other times makes the target extremely uncomfortable.

-Passing as side street stop sign, then stopping an uncomfortable distance into oncoming

traffic just as target is about to arrive at the side street, causing the target to have to slam

on the brakes (this requires Control Center assistance and prompting by walkie-talkie

style cell phone.

-For a CBA vehicle convoy, boxing in the target during a commute, forcing the target to

travel at a lower speed than the target wants to travel. In some locations, the Center will

supply special license plates to CBA vehicles with short words which have special meaning

to the target.

-For a CBA convoy, and where the target is at a location (and time) where traffic is

normally very sparse, cause heavy traffic, forcing the target to notice.

The ultimate vehicle intercept is the staged accident. This can be dangerous and is only

assigned to very senior agents. However, it is possible to stage an accident so only the

target knows it was staged. This is an excellent means of punishment where a target has committed a serious offense specifically against secret services by revealing them

criminality to the public. Staged accidents are done in districts where

police strongly support the operations, so that the CBA driver is protected.

PHYSICAL SABOTAGE

Physical sabotage is an especially effective form of punishment when it is carefully

limited to low value items, below the value where police will take the report seriously.

For example, burning a target's house down, or even stealing an expensive appliance,

would bring official investigators into the picture, so that is not done.

Sabotage producing extreme safety hazards is not suitable for operations,

because of the potential for bringing official investigators to an accident scene. So, while

damaging the brake system of a target's vehicle is not allowed for community-based

agents (CBAs), draining some of the oil, transmission fluid or radiator antifreeze is

allowed, but not all of it. The goal is to make it looks as if the target is negligent in

maintaining fluid levels, and not causing a catastrophic failure that non-targets

might see as sabotage.

It is especially important to apply punishment by way of a large number of small values

sabotage acts because that makes it look like the target is forgetful, exaggerating, or in some cases even delusional if they complain about many cases of small value damage.

The target's associates will simply refuse to believe that anyone, but the target is

responsible.

Sabotage is particularly important in that it lets the target know they are helpless to stop

it, and cannot even complain about it effectively without appearing mentally ill. (The)

organization (is) fortunate in that some people, hearing about sabotage from a

target did the sabotage themselves, "to get attention."

Sabotage is applied at the target's home, workplace, and on their vehicle. This requires

the assistance of locksmiths and alarm technicians. Your local Control Center will supply

this help and will bring specialists in from a distance in the case of rural areas.

Here are some examples of sabotage a community-based agent (CBA) may be assigned to

conduct:

-Entering a vehicle, or home, and changing control and radio settings.

-Replacing window washer fluid with water, destroying the system in winter.

-Scratching the paint on the target's vehicle, scratching furniture and valuables.

-Tire sabotage, from removing some air right up to slashing a sidewall if authorized by the

Center.

-Simulating a break in electric window heater strips.

-Cutting off the 4-way flasher button.

-Removing substantial amounts of oil, transmission fluid or antifreeze but not enough to

cause catastrophic failure.

-Moving things around inside the vehicle to show the target someone got in.

-Unlocking the vehicle and leaving it unlocked, possibly even with the door open.

-Small cuts to car's upholstery.

-Unlocking the target's front or back door and leaving it ajar while the target is away,

even at midnight at New Year for Y2 hour.

-Moving furniture or carpets around fairly frequently to show the target someone was

there.

-Stealing low-value items, especially items like scissors which can be easily misplaced,

keeping them until the target replaces the item, then return the missing item, often in a

place the target checked.

-Stealing important papers, especially those which will cost money to replace.

-Stealing irreplaceable photographs.

-While the target is at work, remove mail from their box and toss it around. Repeatedly

making wall pictures crooked.

-Setting clocks to the wrong time.

-Repeatedly dumping consumable supplies (e.g., coffee) to make the target think they are

no longer capable of managing their supplies well.

-Starting small rips in new clothing, which are widened on repeated visits.

-Ripping crotches out of the target's underwear, or stealing finest underwear, swimsuits,

etc.

-Replacing clothing with equivalent items which are too small for the target, like for children

what target does not have.

-Ironing inside button flags over, making buttoning the shirt or top difficult.

-Carefully working the tip of a knife through seams in any air mattress or cushion the

target may own, including replacements, daily.

-Breaking zippers in clothes and bags, by pulling out a tooth or two.

-Shoving a knife through the soles of waterproof boots.

-At work, removing screws from the target's office chair, or at home dinner table leaving

only one screw of four, left to tilt the table with China.

-At work, damaging or destroying (if not extremely obvious) a target's work from a

the previous day, (for example), the computer is broken again, possibly worse.

-At work, replacing current copies of computer files with an older copy- particularly

serious if the target is a computer programmer.

-At work, where some employees are or can be recruited to be community-based agents,

set up "mistaken deliveries" of heavy goods which block the target's office.

-At work, if the target is responsible for parts of the operation which can be sabotaged,

do so repeatedly just as the target starts eating lunch or is about to leave for home.

-At work where the target is responsible for materials (that) cannot be locked up, sabotage

or with special permission from the Control Center steal the material.

Thefts must be carefully considered and authorized by your local Center, unless you

have authorization, do not steal. One particularly effective type of theft is to remove

small value, but often used items from the target's premises. Once the target has been

observed purchasing a replacement, the item is returned. This not only causes the target

to spend money uselessly, (it also) imposes a feeling of total helplessness on the target.

5. SABOTAGING THE TARGET'S REPUTATION

Sabotaging the target's reputation- and all that goes with it, such as ability to earn a

living, business and personal relationships- is an incredibly special operations category. Newer

community-based agents will not be assigned to "engineer" the method, but will assist in

passing "rumors," which are the main means of destroying a target's public image.

"Rumors" consist mainly of lies. However, to secure cooperation of specific

members of the community to participate in the punishment phase, additional

information keyed to appeal to the patriotic or community service sense of such

community members may be used as well. As mentioned earlier, the organization has many top psychologists and psychiatrists on permanent staff at headquarters, and some

in larger population centers. It is their responsibility to design the campaign to destroy

the target's reputation.

These people listed below can be approached and given information which will cause

them to make the target's association with them uncomfortable, or break off all contact

with the target.

-Business contacts.

-Supervisors.

-Co-workers.

-Casual social contacts, such as clubs a target may be a member of, or a group that

frequents a bar where the target is a patron.

-Friends.

-Local fraternal organizations- they are motivated by the public service, and are an

excellent source of assistance in keeping the target under surveillance, and participating

in the punishment phase as well.

-Store staff at places the target shops.

-Monitoring newspapers in your area for letters to the editor regarding activities. Most

editors and many reporters have been recruited and are willing to assist in keeping the

important work of monitoring and neutralizing quiet, but occasionally, a letter to the

editor will slip through. In this case, comments like "Someone is not taking their medication" are not an appropriate response. Transcribe and forward such a letter to the

editor to the supervisor, along with your proposed response. The supervisor may edit

your response and will assist in ensuring your response are printed.

-Your supervisor will have staff monitoring upcoming talk show appearances by targets.

While most talk show hosts, even those sympathetic to targets, have received

discrediting information and often will not host targets, some targets do manage to get

on the air. In this case, your supervisor will assign you to call in to the show, and instruct

you as to appropriate things to say, such as rebutting the target's claims, pretending to be

a target calling and making "wacko" statements such as "UFOs are harassing me," or

pulling the discussion away from real activities and to something like "media mind

control."

-Agents who have excellent persuasive communication skills can be assigned, with careful

coaching and preparation from supervisors, to pretend to be a target and get on talk

shows known to air targets as the guest. These opportunities are great ways to discredit

targets by talking about UFOs, things like black helicopters following you, foil beanies,

satellites "parked" just above your home, and events normally considered

"paranormal" like seeing (things that) appear and disappear. These discrediting topics must be a total surprise to the host, only mentioned after the show is in progress.

-CBA can "casually" describe the "odd behavior" exhibited by the target because of

around the clock activities to the target's neighbors. The idea is to focus the neighbors'

attention to the target's behavior, hinting that the target is mentally ill. This is

easy once the target has developed suspicion that "everyone is out to get" him or her.

It is a special "honor" for CBAs to be chosen for target discreditation work.

7. TRADE-RELATED PUNISHMENT

This section will give some examples of ways community-based agents (CBAs) with

specific trades or situations in the community can apply deniable punishment to targets.

-Underground utility crews, where the management has been recruited, schedule messy,

noisy maintenance at the target's home (or business if the target runs a business). This

can include having the street torn up for extended periods, or repeatedly. Funding for

unneeded work is available from headquarters. Taxi drivers can delay arriving when

called by the target, especially when going to the airport.

-Bus drivers have leeway, in nasty weather for example, to stop one stop away from

awaiting target and wait there for 5 minutes, to "get back on

schedule." This can also cause a target to miss connections with the next bus or train. This is especially effective when the target, exposed to severe weather, can see the bus waiting

up the street for no apparent reason, or not stopping at all at your bus stop.

-Repair trades people can keep "getting it wrong" necessitating many recalls, be late, be

messy, over-bill the target, and even damage things which were OK. This is especially

effective in the automobile repair trade.

-Medical lab technicians can substitute blood samples, or otherwise falsify results making

The target appears to have absolutely no reason for their complaints.

-Police can frequently pull the target over for frivolous reasons.

-Telephone and cable TV technicians can re-route legitimate calls to the target's number

in large numbers, and this will cause the target to get incredibly angry with these totally

innocent callers.

-Store staff where the target shops frequently can be instructed to remove items the

target is known to need when a target is known to be coming. Store management can

stop ordering a target's favorite items.

-Restaurants and food delivery services can tell the target they are out of an item known

to be a favorite of a target.

The key to successful punishment by trades people is that while the target is highly likely to

know they are being punished, these punishment acts must appear to the public

as "life's normal breaks."

8. TARGET'S HOME

Punishing the target at the target's (home) is essential for effectiveness of secret service

operations. If the target were punished in the community but was allowed sanctuary in

their home, the creation of a "prison without walls" would not be complete. One of the

very first things the Control Center (CC) will arrange is for homes or apartments adjacent

to the target's home to be occupied by both community-based agents (CBAs) and

members in the Electronic Operations manual. Because operations are conducted 24/7 in

shifts, homes, and apartments which are leased or owned by staff are not used as

dwellings. The lease or deed will bear either an entirely false name, or the name of a

senior staff member whose actual home will be at a different location.

Some adjacent homes or apartments are occupied by neighbors of the target who have

offered to cooperate in punishment of the target. The initial contact of neighbors to

determine their willingness to cooperate is done by senior staff, and incentives to

cooperate are often tendered. Here are some commonly used punishment activities

which are conducted both by CBAs and cooperating neighbors of the target. Activities are

rotated among the choices, but at least one of them is applied daily:

-Noise. Noise must be of a type which the public deems "normal." Remember that the goal is to have the target aware they are being punished, but not be able to

convince anyone else that that is the case. Observe local noise curfews, but plenty of

punishment can occur outside noise curfew times. The target must not have easy cause to

involve law enforcement. Examples:

-Start leaf blower, times precisely when the target attempts to enjoy their yard, or when

EC operators cue the CBA that the target is trying to nap.

-Loud music from neighboring home. This is an excellent action, as it is common. Time it

so, every time the target opens a window the music starts. The timing makes the point it

is intentional punishment. EC operator can apply music in adjacent apartments with

exceptionally powerful bass, directed at the target's unit.

-Frequent squealing of tires near target's home.

-In apartments, frequent drilling into a scrap of wood or masonry held against the target's

wall, floors or ceiling as if "working." Alternatively, hammering. Especially effective when

cued by EC operators that the target is attempting to nap.

-Tossing golf or tennis balls against the target's home when the target is known to be

trying to fall asleep. Ideal for cooperating with neighbor children.

-Frequent use of sirens near the target's home. Many emergencies' services employees

have a powerful sense of community service and willingness to cooperate in this, or by

people posing as Jehovah's Witnesses.

-Knocking on the door for frivolous/nonsensical/wrong address reasons. Especially

effective when the target is in bed or having a meal.

-Trash. Leave trash in the target's yard. Frequently, but CC staff will assist in scheduling

this so that the target cannot quite have a case on which law enforcement will act.

-Terrifying the target's pet. This requires entry while the target is away from home for an

extended period and must be scheduled by CC. Electronic Corps (EC) operators can render

a dog or cat passive for safe entry of the community-based agents, by electromagnetic

beam.

-Wounding or killing the target's pet. Rarely used, scheduled when the target has acted in

a way to deserve special punishment, like divulging the name of a criminally acting

secret agent.

-Killing domestic animals or wildlife and leaving them on the target's doorstep. Scheduled

when the target has acted in a way to deserve special punishment.

-Where the target owns substantial land, noxious activities can be arranged and built for

next to the property. In one case, a dump, an auto racetrack, and a prison were built

adjacent to a target who owned a large farm in an area of natural beauty. While this is

rare, it does illustrate commitment to delivering punishment to those "deserving" of it.

-Cooperating police departments can visibly watch the target's home. Possibly being parked in front of the home when the target returns, repeatedly.

Police officers who refuse to take complaint of harassment and sabotage of the target,

who they label "disturbed" – really are NOT allowed to make diagnoses, as only medical

doctors can do but may get a raise- price- for their unlawfulness afterward. Police follow

orders by e.g., Stay Behind, Secret Military-led organization, created by the CIA after WWII

in NATO countries. They give orders in secrecy to police, media, legal system, and judges,

etc. Thus, being above parliaments and governments as demonstrated, for example, in

Norway when in 1957 the Chief of "Stay Behind" Sven Ollestad gave the security code of

Norway to MI6 (British Intelligence) in the UK acting on his own! "We must trust our

allies," he had said. Today, the security code of Norway is kept in Wales. Originally, Stay

Behind was created with good intentions to fight communism. Today it is out of control,

and a new, much bigger Stay Behind 2 is active in Norway. The Stay Behind logo

resembles the NATO logo.

In Italy, Stay Behind was called Gladio 2 and dealt with terrorism secretly in Western

Europe. It was responsible, for example, for the kidnapping and killing of Prime Minister

Aldo Moro in 1978, while the blame was pinned on the Red Brigade. Today, enemies are

communists and NATO (are the) opposition.

On November 22, 1990, the European Union forbade Operation Gladio, but although

Norway follows most EU decisions, this one is omitted. Italy and Belgium had terror

actions by Stay Behind, and when the organizations (ceased to exist, the terror operations

also ceased to exist). In Norway, Stay Behind is called E14. What was its role in Norway's

terror actions, if any? Some have tried to get control of Norwegian Stay Behind (armies)

already years ago. Who are the back men giving orders to those "officially" in charge?

The late Chief Medical Officer of northern Finland, and Targeted Individual, Dr. Rauni-

Leena Lukanen Kilde

Appendix 1. Key Words and Phrases from the Organized Gang Stalking Manual Above

Key words to chapter 18.

Major operational components of organization:

-Community-based agent (CBA)

-Electronic Corps (EC)

-Electronic Operations Manual

-electromagnetic beam

-Control Center (CC)

-On-Site-Supervisor (OSS)

Field Operations People

-Psychologists/Psychiatrists

-Advanced computer communications systems and computer programs

Elements of (secret service) gang stalking operations:

-Surveillance is foundation of all operations

-Operations are "active surveillance type"

-Passive surveillance, watching the target covertly, to obtain information

-Community-Based Agents- CBA

-Every act of punishment is DENIABLE

-Advanced technology enables heavy punishment (when) the target is in their home,

silently through walls.

-Electronic Corps (EC) members get specialized electronic punishment training

-Advanced electronic surveillance

-This manual

-Field operations people

-Psychologists are the key to find ways to maximize feelings of stress and hopelessness in

target, and degrading target's health.

-CBAs are given cell phone number for reporting target actions and movement to local

Control Center (CC)

-The Center (CC) always has the target's position monitored.

-Electronic Corps (EC) has through-the-wall surveillance and punishment equipment

-On-site-supervisor (OSS) will give hand signals

-Computer programs predict exactly when and where a target will be as they move

through the community.

-OSS has a special means of receiving instant, silent instructions for the Center.

-Intercepts are where CBAs appear to "just coincidentally" cross paths, on foot or by

vehicle with the target.

-The ultimate vehicle intercept is the staged accident... excellent means of punishment where target has committed serious offense specifically against secret services by

revealing their criminality to the public.

-Sabotage lets the target know they are helpless to stop harassment

-Thefts must be authorized by local Control Center

-Sabotage of target's reputation- is special operations category- done by spreading

rumors, consisting of lies. The goal is to keep negative information about the

target flowing through the community.

-The organization has many top psychologists and psychiatrists on permanent staff at

headquarters. Their job is to design campaigns to destroy a target's reputation.

- "Incentives" are offered to get neighbors, friends, community members to cooperate

-The "Organization has powerful silent support of operations by the justice and

psychiatric systems

-Monitoring newspapers for letters to the editor regarding these activities.

-Monitoring talk radio show appearances by targets.

-Repair trades people can damage items (cars, travel trailers, etc.) of targets and/or

overbill targets

-Police can frequently pull the target over for frivolous reasons

-Punishing the target at the target's home is essential for effective secret service

operations to create a "prison without walls."

Operations are conducted 24/7 in shifts

-Control Center (CC) will arrange for homes or apartments adjacent to the target's home to be occupied by both community-based agents (CBA) and members in the Electrical

Operations manual.

-Electronic Corp (EC) operators can render a dog or cat passive for safe entry of the

community-based agents, by electromagnetic beam.

Political Objectives Operations and Activities

Terrorism: The U.S. and its allies may engage in actions that terrorize civilian populations to achieve political objectives. The Department of Defense (DOD) acknowledges: "Some irregular warfare (IW) activities, such as terrorism and transnational crime, violate international law. U.S. law and national policy prohibit U.S. military forces or other government agencies (OGAs) from engaging in or supporting such activities. However, because our adversaries use terrorism and transnational criminal activities against the interests of the United States and its partners, these activities are included... as examples of the range of operations and activities that can be conducted as part of IW."

Fourth Generation Warfare (4GW): 4GW is a form of political and information warfare waged by states or other entities against civilian populations. It involves the entire society, including civilians and the military, in targeting adversaries who are often labeled as "domestic state enemies," "insurgents," extremists, non-state actors, or citizen "terrorists"—anyone who values national sovereignty or poses a perceived threat to the state's interests.

In this context, even those who disseminate information contrary to the state's "national security" interests may be considered enemies. The New War's goal is to induce the psychological collapse of these new enemies using a combination of tactics. Defeating them involves the synchronized use of non-lethal directed energy weapons, isolation, deprivation, and psychological operations (PsyOps) against targeted individuals and groups.

4GW is closely related to unconventional warfare (UW), irregular warfare (IW), asymmetric warfare (AW), low-intensity conflict (LIC), military operations other than war (MOOTW), and network-centric warfare (NCW). This war involves international and interagency cooperation, incorporating military, federal, and local law enforcement, non-governmental organizations (NGOs), intergovernmental organizations (IGOs), the civilian population, and private government contractors. This multinational force (MNF), involving NATO and the UN, is referred to as civilian-military operations (CMO).

Insurgents: Insurgents are individuals or groups who seek to persuade the populace to accept political change. These enemies do not necessarily resort to violence; their methods may be nonviolent. They are often individuals not under government control who oppose the established leadership. They may be targeted for actions they might take in the future, including nonviolent protests, which can lead to them being labeled as terrorists. These individuals may align themselves with nationalism.

Civilian-Military Operations (CMO): CMO combines military forces, federal agencies, NGOs, civilian organizations, and authorities with the civilian population. CMO is employed in friendly, neutral, or hostile operational areas, including populated civilian areas where no other military activity occurs.

It addresses domestic threats in the New War. The controlling faction of these PsyOp/CMO activities includes the military, federal agencies, NGOs, regional organizations, and international organizations that collaborate with civil authorities. In the U.S., the controlling faction includes FEMA, DOJ, CIA, and other federal agencies (FBI, DHS, etc.). Civilians are used as irregular forces, and CMOs are interagency and global in nature, playing a significant role in Homeland Security.

Civilian-Military Operations Centers (CMOC): CMOCs are established in civilian sectors to facilitate the exchange of ideas. These can be physical meeting places or virtual networks. Representatives from the military, NGOs, private sector, and local officials attend daily meetings to discuss ongoing campaigns against domestic threats within the operational area.

C4ISR (Command, Control, Communications, Computers, Intelligence, Surveillance, and Reconnaissance): C4ISR systems are crucial for battlespace monitoring, awareness, command intent, and information systems management. These centers, which can be mobile, stationary, or virtual, are used by various military branches. For example, the Navy and Marines use ForceNet, the Air Force uses Command Control Constellation (C2 Constellation), and the Army uses LandWarNet and WIN-T. All C4ISR systems are connected to the Global Information Grid (GIG).

Cognitive Radio (CR): A Cognitive Radio is an intelligent device with artificial intelligence (AI) capabilities. It is aware of itself, the user's needs, and the environment, capable of understanding and learning. Programs like the Adaptive Cognition-Enhanced Radio Teams (ACERT) and Situation Aware Protocols in Edge Network Technologies (SAPIENT), supported by DARPA, contributed to CR development.

Global Information Grid (GIG): Developed partially by the MITRE Corporation, GIG is the DOD's global C4ISR unit for netwar. It can rapidly locate and target adversaries anywhere on Earth, using directed energy weapons (DEW) and other forms of electronic warfare (EW). GIG connects to all communications systems used by coalition and allied forces. Some of the directed energy weapons developed are:

Laser Weapons

Laser Weapon System (LaWS) : Deployed aboard the USS Ponce, LaWS is a solid-state laser weapon designed for use against small boat threats and aerial drones. It uses a high-energy laser to destroy or disable targets.

Active Denial System (ADS) : A non-lethal laser weapon developed by the U.S. military that emits millimeter waves to cause a painful but non-injurious heating sensation on the skin. It is intended for crowd control and area denial.

High Energy Laser (HEL) Systems:

Various HEL systems have been developed for potential use in missile defense and countering aerial threats. These include the Army's High Energy Laser Tactical Vehicle Demonstrator (HEL TVD) and the Navy's Laser Weapon System (LaWS) for ship defense.

Microwave Weapons

Active Denial System (ADS) : As mentioned, the ADS uses microwave technology to create a heating effect on the skin, causing discomfort to disperse crowds or deter intruders without causing permanent injury.

High-Powered Microwave (HPM) Weapons: These weapons generate intense microwave pulses that can disrupt or destroy electronic equipment. The U.S. military has researched HPM systems for applications such as disabling enemy electronics and protecting assets from electronic attacks.

Airborne Laser (ABL) : ABL was a research program designed to use a high-energy laser mounted on a modified Boeing 747 to intercept and destroy ballistic missiles in their boost phase. Although it demonstrated some capability, the program was eventually canceled due to technical and cost challenges.

Space-Based Laser (SBL) : The SBL program aimed to develop a space-based platform with a high-energy laser to intercept ballistic missiles. However, it faced numerous technical and budgetary hurdles and was eventually canceled.

Other DEW Concepts

Laser-Induced Plasma Channel (LIPC) : An experimental technology that creates a plasma channel in the air through which a laser beam can travel. This technology has potential applications for long-range directed energy weapons.

Free Electron Lasers (FELs) : FELs are a type of laser weapon that uses a beam of electrons traveling through a magnetic field to generate high-energy lasers. They offer potential advantages for high-energy output and beam quality but remain largely in the experimental phase.

Development and Deployment

While several directed energy weapons have been developed and assessed, many are still in experimental or developmental stages. The primary focus has been on increasing the power, reliability, and accuracy of these systems, as well as addressing technical challenges such as power requirements and beam control. Directed energy weapons represent a growing area of military technology with potential applications in missile defense, electronic warfare, and non-lethal crowd control.

Global War on Terror (GWOT): GWOT involves the use of second, third, and fourth-generation warfare to achieve the political and military objectives of the American Empire and the New World Order.

Information Operations (IO): Also known as "cyber war," "information warfare," or "network-centric warfare," IO refers to activities that involve conveying information. In the context of government and military use, the DOD defines IO as: "The integrated employment of core capabilities—electronic warfare, computer network operations, psychological operations, military deception, and operations security—influence, disrupt, corrupt, or usurp adversarial human and automated decision-making while protecting our own." This form of warfare is often used to influence and gain the support of the population.

Information Warfare (IW): According to U.S. Military and Defense Contractors, the "new enemy" utilizes various information technologies, such as computers, the internet, fax machines, cell phones, and public media, to advance their objectives. Publications describe these activities as "netwar," "information operations," "information warfare," or "information attacks." The target of information warfare is the human mind. As Professor George J. Stein stated in "Information Warfare," the battle is fundamentally for control of the mind.

This new war revolves around psychological influence and the struggle for the minds of the population, making it an information war.

Information Warfare

Infrasonic and ultrasonic weapons, though traditionally associated with physical effects, have significant applications in information warfare, particularly in psychological operations, perception management, and disinformation. Infrasonic weapons, which operate at frequencies below human hearing, can induce feelings of unease, anxiety, or physical discomfort without being consciously detected. This makes them valuable in psychological operations aimed at creating fear or disorientation, thereby making targets more susceptible to influence. Similarly, ultrasonic weapons, which emit high-frequency sound waves above the range of hearing, can cause physical discomfort or pain, contributing to cognitive disruption. These effects can be exploited to disrupt communication and amplify the impact of misinformation or propaganda, making individuals more vulnerable to manipulation.

The subtle and often undetectable nature of infrasonic and ultrasonic weapons adds to their utility in information warfare, particularly in scenarios where it is difficult for targets to identify the source of their discomfort. This ambiguity can be leveraged to sow doubt, create false attributions, and manipulate public perception. For example, these weapons could be used covertly to create chaos, which is then blamed on another party, undermining credibility and fostering misinformation. When used in conjunction with traditional information warfare tactics—such as cyber-attacks or propaganda—these weapons can amplify the overall impact by disorienting populations and making them more receptive to fear-based messaging. The psychosomatic effects they induce can lead to widespread health concerns, which can be further exploited through media and social networks to destabilize societies or weaken resolve. Thus, infrasonic, and ultrasonic weapons serve as powerful tools in the arsenal of information warfare, enhancing the effectiveness of psychological and perceptual manipulation.

Infrasonic and Ultrasonic Weapons:

Infrasonic and ultrasonic generators, also known as emitters and VLF modulators, have evolved in sophistication and application over the years. A modern example includes the use of the "Long Range Acoustic Device" (LRAD), a crowd-control tool deployed by police forces during protests in the United States and elsewhere. The LRAD emits a high-pitched sound that can cause pain, disorientation, and even hearing damage, forcing people to disperse. Similar technologies have been used by the military to ward off pirates in the Gulf of Aden and by cruise ships as a deterrent against boarding.

Russia's continued development of infrasonic and ultrasonic weapons has reportedly led to advanced versions that can target individuals with extreme precision. These devices can induce a range of physiological and psychological effects, including pain, nausea, and feelings of dread. In recent conflicts, such as the ongoing unrest in Ukraine, there have been unverified reports of these weapons being used in urban warfare to break the will of soldiers and civilians alike.

Infrasound:

Infrasound, within the Extremely Low Frequency (ELF) range, remains a powerful tool due to its ability to travel through structures and over long distances. Modern examples of infrasound applications include its use in military and police operations for crowd control. For instance, during large-scale protests in Hong Kong in 2019, there were allegations (though not confirmed by authorities) of infrasound devices being used to disperse crowds without leaving visible injuries, causing disorientation and discomfort among the demonstrators.

Additionally, researchers have been exploring the potential use of infrasound in disrupting drone operations by interfering with their sensors, which rely on precise frequency detection for navigation and communication. This could offer a non-lethal method to counter the increasing threat posed by unmanned aerial vehicles in both military and civilian contexts.

Microwave Hearing:

Microwave hearing, or "Voice to Skull" (V2K) technology, has seen advancements that make it more portable and effective.

Microwave hearing, commonly referred to as "Voice to Skull" (V2K) technology, is a form of directed energy technology that uses microwave signals to transmit sound directly into a person's skull, bypassing the traditional auditory system.

The concept of microwave hearing is rooted in the Frey Effect, named after Dr. Allan H. Frey, who first described this phenomenon in the 1960s. This effect demonstrated that microwaves could induce the perception of sound in humans, laying the groundwork for subsequent developments in V2K technology.

Notable examples include the U.S. military's S-Quad device, which projects sound into an individual's head using microwave frequencies, and the MEDUSA (Mob Excess Deterrent Using Silent Audio) concept weapon developed by the U.S. Navy. MEDUSA was intended for crowd control by projecting sounds directly into a person's head, potentially creating the illusion of internal voices to disorient targets.

V2K technology has been explored for a variety of uses, particularly in psychological operations (PsyOps) where it could be employed to manipulate, confuse, or disorient individuals or groups. By projecting voices or sounds directly into a target's head, the technology can create the impression of internal thoughts or hallucinations, influencing behavior.

It also has potential applications in non-lethal crowd control, where authorities could use it to disperse crowds or disorient individuals without causing physical harm. Additionally, V2K could be utilized in interrogation and coercion settings, inducing confusion or fear to mentally pressure detainees. There is also theoretical potential for covert communication, allowing messages to be delivered directly to individuals without detection by others, useful in espionage or special operations.

The development of microwave hearing technology has primarily been undertaken by military and defense contractors, with companies like Raytheon and Lockheed Martin playing significant roles in researching and developing these advanced systems.

The Defense Advanced Research Projects Agency (DARPA), the U.S. Department of Defense's research arm, has also funded various projects related to directed energy and microwave technologies, including V2K capabilities. Independent researchers and laboratories have contributed to the foundational understanding of how this technology works and its potential applications.

The primary users of V2K technology have been the U.S. military, particularly in the context of psychological operations, crowd control, and non-lethal weaponry. Some law enforcement agencies have shown interest in non-lethal directed energy weapons, including V2K, for use in crowd control or hostage situations, although deployment at the civilian level is less documented.

There are also claims and theories suggesting that intelligence agencies may have used V2K technology for covert operations, including psychological warfare and the manipulation of individuals. However, such uses are often shrouded in secrecy and lack official confirmation, contributing to ongoing debates about the ethical implications and potential misuse of this technology.

A recent example of this technology in action is the "Havana Syndrome" incident, where U.S. diplomats in Cuba and China reported hearing unexplained sounds followed by symptoms such as headaches, nausea, and memory loss. While the exact cause remains debated, many experts suspect that a form of microwave energy, potentially used as a weapon, was responsible for these effects. This incident has led to increased concern over the use of microwave hearing in modern espionage and covert operations, where it could be employed to disorient or psychologically manipulate targets without leaving any physical evidence.

Non-Lethal Weapons (NLW):

The use of non-lethal weapons has become more prevalent in recent years, particularly in the context of law enforcement and military operations. Modern examples include the deployment of tasers and rubber bullets by police forces during civil unrest, such as the protests following the killing of George Floyd in 2020. These weapons are intended to incapacitate individuals temporarily without causing permanent harm, though their misuse has led to significant injuries and controversy.

Another advanced NLW is the Active Denial System (ADS), often referred to as the "heat ray." This directed-energy weapon emits a beam of millimeter waves that rapidly heats the surface of the skin, causing an intense burning sensation that forces people to flee. The U.S. military has evaluated ADS in various scenarios, including crowd control and perimeter defense. Although its use in combat zones has been limited due to ethical concerns, ADS is a significant leap forward in non-lethal weaponry.

Neuroimaging Devices:

Remote Neural Monitoring (RNM) and Remote Neural Manipulation are at the forefront of surveillance and psychological operations. Today, neuroimaging technology is being developed and evaluated for use in both medical and security fields. For example, law enforcement agencies in some countries are exploring the use of RNM to monitor the brain activity of suspects, potentially identifying intent or deceit. Additionally, there are concerns about the possible misuse of this technology by authoritarian regimes to control dissidents or by corporations to manipulate consumer behavior.

One speculative yet concerning example is the potential for neural devices to be used in enhancing interrogation techniques, where the interrogation subject's neural responses could be monitored and influenced in real-time, making it difficult for them to lie or resist questioning.

Political Warfare and Psychological Operations (PsyOp):

Political warfare, especially through PsyOp, has become more sophisticated with the advent of social media and big data analytics. A modern example is the alleged Russian interference in the 2016 U.S. presidential election, where a combination of cyber operations, social media manipulation, and misinformation campaigns were used to influence public opinion and sow discord. These tactics are part of a broader strategy of "hybrid warfare," which blends conventional military force with unconventional methods like PsyOp.

Another contemporary example is the extensive use of psychological operations in the ongoing conflict in Ukraine. Both Russian and Ukrainian forces have employed PsyOp through social media platforms, spreading disinformation, propaganda, and demoralizing content to influence both the domestic and international perception of the conflict. This includes deepfake videos, fake news stories, and targeted harassment campaigns aimed at undermining the morale of soldiers and civilians on both sides.

The U.S. military has also been active in this domain, developing sophisticated PsyOp capabilities to influence public opinion in conflict zones like Iraq and Afghanistan. These operations often involve the dissemination of tailored messages through local media, social networks, and even text messages to sway the attitudes and behaviors of specific target audiences.

These modern examples illustrate how technologies and tactics that were once theoretical or experimental are now being deployed in real-world scenarios, often with profound and far-reaching consequences. Early PsyOp research was done by a small private network of think tanks, foundations, and academic institutions, which went into partnership with government agencies and kept most of the results of their studies secret. Some of the institutions that conducted these studies were known to be subversive. Thus, much of the modern PsyOp was built by a small group of private interests, using the social sciences to install a global

government. Some of these are the exact same groups promoting the use of PsyOp on

civilians.

Rumor Campaigns- used by PsyOp units to isolate TIs. Primary elements include the

source, the rumor, and the receiver-repeater (R2).

Similarly, the US Marine Corps document, "Multiple-Service Concept for Irregular

Warfare" (2006) states: "frightening the population into inactivity is sufficient to

(achieve) our goals."

TPD – Tactical PsyOp Detachment- team of about thirteen personnel with a captain and staff

sergeant. It is comprised of several TPT (Tactical PsyOp Teams) and provides tactical

PsyOp support to brigade and battalion-sized units in support of Special Forces. TPT

conducts mission assessment, determines distribution priorities, and tracks the various

products that have been distributed throughout the AO. All teams maintain contact with

each other. And the TPD is in constant communication with other forces such as the

TPDD, POTF, or TPT during the entire operation.

TPT- Tactical PsyOp Team- small group including team leader, his assistant, and a PsyOp

specialist.

CNO- Computer Network Operations- aka NW Ops, or network operations/NetOps) are

information warfare attacks used to deny, deceive, degrade, and disrupt networks and

computers used by the enemy. These are used in conjunction with PO (PsyOps) and EW

(electronic warfare). This includes destruction of hardware and software (degrading,

attacking) and spoofing (deceiving). The battlespace includes the internet. Internet

applications that can convey PsyOp messages include email, websites, and chat rooms.

When a TI goes online, they are entering the battlespace.

Web spoofing allows an attacker to create a copy of the worldwide web. The Air Force

mentioned that an enemy's internet could be spoofed to conceal one of its weather

attacks: "Spoofing options create virtual weather in the enemy's sensory and information

systems, making it more likely for them to make decisions producing results of our

choosing rather than theirs."

DEW- Directed Energy Weapons- used to damage or destroy people, equipment, and

facilities, include microwave, millimeter waves, lasers, bright lights, holographic

projections, and acoustic weapons (audible, infrasound, and ultrasound). These weapons

are silent and traceless. They cause a variety of effects, including tiredness, dizziness,

nausea, vomiting, abdominal pain, convulsions, epileptic seizures, temporary paralysis, vibration of internal organs, cooking of organs, cataracts, burning sensation on the skin,

hyperthermia (heating of body), headaches, loss of short-term memory, interruption of

cognitive processes, cardiac arrest, and cancer.

These weapons can easily pass through most unshielded structures.

In their "Electronic Warfare" publication, DOD defines DEW as: "DE (directed energy) is an

umbrella term covering technologies that produce a beam of concentrated EM energy or

atomic or subatomic particles. A DE weapon is a system using DE primarily as a direct

means to damage or destroy adversary equipment, facilities, and personnel. DE warfare is

military action involving the use of DE weapons, devices, and countermeasures to either

cause direct damage or destruction of adversary equipment, facilities, and personnel, or

to determine, exploit, reduce, or prevent hostile use of the EMS through damage,

destruction, and disruption."

DEW includes microwaves, lasers, bright lights, holographic projections, and acoustics.

The two basic types of DEWs include microwaves and lasers. (Wavelengths of lasers are

about 10,000 times smaller than microwaves). Both are part of the electromagnetic

spectrum. The two main types of microwave weapons are millimeter wave devices such

as the Active Denial System (ADS) and the electromagnetic bomb (e-bomb, which is the

emission of a non-nuclear electromagnetic explosion or pulse).

DEW travel at the speed of light, are surgically accurate, can operate in all weather, are

scalable, are silent and invisible (offering plausible deniability), their energy can pass

through walls at distances of hundreds of meters to miles, and have long distance

projection (tens of miles).

These weapons are mounted on platforms which can be a missile, aircraft, ship, vehicle,

suitcase, radio, etc.

Weapons

Basic Principles

Electromagnetic Radiation: RF weapons generate electromagnetic radiation, which consists of oscillating electric and magnetic fields. This radiation travels through space at the speed of light and can be tuned to specific frequencies within the radio frequency spectrum, ranging from a few kilohertz (kHz) to several gigahertz (GHz).

Focused Energy:

RF weapons typically focus this energy into a directed beam or pulse. The energy is concentrated to maximize its impact on the target, whether it is electronic equipment or living organisms.

Types of RF Weapons and Their Operation

RF – Radio Frequency Weapons

Radio frequency (RF) weapons are a class of directed-energy weapons that utilize electromagnetic radiation within the radio frequency spectrum to disrupt, damage, or incapacitate electronic equipment, or to affect human targets in various ways. These weapons have diverse applications across military, law enforcement, and other government sectors. High-Power Microwave (HPM) weapons, for example, emit bursts of microwave energy capable of disrupting or damaging electronic systems by inducing electrical currents or overheating components. Militaries use HPM weapons to disable enemy electronics, such as radar systems and communication networks, without causing physical damage to infrastructure. In contrast, law enforcement might use HPM weapons to disable vehicles or drones during high-risk situations, like car chases, offering a non-lethal alternative.

Another RF weapon is the Active Denial System (ADS), a non-lethal technology that uses millimeter-wave radiation to create an intense burning sensation on the skin of a target without causing permanent injury. The U.S. military has deployed ADS for crowd control in conflict zones or during peacekeeping missions, allowing them to disperse large groups without inflicting lasting harm. While ADS could be used in law enforcement for riot control or area denial, its application in civilian contexts is controversial due to ethical concerns. RF jammers are another tool, emitting radio waves that disrupt communication signals, such as cell phone or GPS signals. The military employs RF jammers to prevent enemy communications, disable remote-controlled improvised explosive devices (IEDs), and protect convoys by disrupting potential threats. Law enforcement agencies might use RF jammers in situations like hostage rescues or bomb threats, though their use is heavily regulated to prevent interference with civilian communications.

Electromagnetic Pulse (EMP) weapons generate bursts of electromagnetic radiation that disable electronic devices by overloading their circuits. These weapons are designed to incapacitate an enemy's electronic infrastructure, including communication networks and power grids, without causing direct harm to people or buildings. EMP weapons might be considered in extreme scenarios, such as national security threats, where disabling an adversary's critical infrastructure is necessary to prevent a larger attack. Directed Energy RF Weapons focus RF energy in a beam to target specific electronics or personnel, and depending on the frequency and power, they can disrupt electronics or cause discomfort and damage to living tissues. The military explores directed energy RF weapons to disable enemy drones, vehicles, or communication equipment at a distance, part of ongoing research into next-generation warfare technologies. Law enforcement could use these weapons to disable vehicles or drones during pursuits or incapacitate hostile individuals in non-lethal scenarios.

Microwave Hearing, also known as "Voice to Skull" (V2K) technology, is a more experimental application that uses microwaves to send audio signals directly into a person's skull, making them perceive sounds or voices. This technology, which works by slightly heating tissues inside the head to create audible voices, has been considered for psychological operations (psyops) to confuse or demoralize enemy troops. There are reports of its exploration for use in crowd control or interrogation settings, although its effectiveness and ethical implications remain heavily debated. Finally, Tactical RF Weapons are portable or vehicle-mounted devices designed for short-range applications, like disrupting the electronics of vehicles or drones. The military might use these weapons in urban combat or to protect high-value assets from drone attacks, providing a way to neutralize threats without collateral damage. Law enforcement could use tactical

RF weapons to safely disable drones used for illegal activities or stop vehicles during high-speed chases.

These various RF weapons highlight the broad range of applications for radio frequency energy in military and law enforcement contexts. While they offer significant strategic advantages, their development and use also raise critical ethical, legal, and safety concerns.

Radio frequency (RF) weapons operate by harnessing electromagnetic radiation in the radio frequency spectrum to achieve various effects on electronic systems or human targets. Here's a detailed explanation of how RF weapons work:

High-Power Microwave (HPM) Weapons:

How They Work: HPM weapons emit short bursts of microwave radiation at high power levels. This radiation induces electrical currents in electronic circuits, causing them to overheat and malfunction. The microwaves can also disrupt communication systems and radar by interfering with their signals.

Applications: The primary use is to disable or damage enemy electronic equipment, such as radar systems, communication networks, and missile guidance systems. HPM weapons can be deployed from aircraft, ground-based systems, or even drones.

Active Denial System (ADS):

How It Works: ADS operates using millimeter-wave radiation, which is absorbed by the skin's surface. The energy causes a rapid heating of the skin's outer layer, creating an intense but non-lethal burning sensation. This sensation prompts people to move away from the source of the radiation to avoid discomfort.

Applications: The ADS is used for crowd control, area denial, and dispersal of groups. It is designed to create a strong deterrent effect without causing permanent injury, making it suitable for use in conflict zones or during peacekeeping missions.

RF Jammers:

How They Work: RF jammers emit signals across a broad range of frequencies to overwhelm or block incoming signals. By broadcasting noise or interference on the same frequencies used by communication devices, RF jammers can prevent devices from receiving or transmitting data.

Applications: RF jammers are used to disrupt enemy communications, disable remote-controlled improvised explosive devices (IEDs), and block GPS or cell phone signals. They are commonly used in military operations and can also be employed by law enforcement in specific scenarios.

Electromagnetic Pulse (EMP) Weapons:

How They Work: EMP weapons generate a burst of electromagnetic radiation that causes a rapid and widespread surge of electrical energy in electronic devices. This surge can overload circuits, damage components, and disrupt electronic systems.

Applications: EMP weapons aim to incapacitate an enemy's electronic infrastructure, including power grids, communication systems, and military hardware. They can be delivered through explosive devices or specialized equipment and are considered for scenarios where disabling technology is necessary without physical destruction.

Directed Energy RF Weapons:

How They Work: Directed energy RF weapons focus RF energy into a precise beam or pulse. Depending on the frequency and power of the beam, it can disrupt or damage electronic systems or cause discomfort and harm to individuals. The beam can be adjusted to target specific devices or areas.

Applications: These weapons are explored for disabling enemy drones, vehicles, or communication equipment from a distance. They represent next-generation technology for military operations and may also have potential law enforcement applications.

Microwave Hearing/V2K Technology:

How It Works: This technology uses microwaves to induce audible sounds directly into a person's head. By modulating microwave signals, the technology causes slight thermal effects in the auditory nerves, creating the perception of sound without external speakers.

Applications: Though experimental, this technology has been considered for psychological operations, crowd control, or interrogation scenarios. It aims to influence or confuse targets by making them hear voices or sounds, though its effectiveness and ethical implications are still debated.

Corrolation between COINTELPRO and Operation Gladio

Operation Gladio was a clandestine NATO operation that emerged in the aftermath of World War II as part of a broader network of "stay-behind" operations across Western Europe. These operations were designed to prepare for the possibility of a Soviet invasion during the Cold War, with the intent of fostering resistance movements behind enemy lines. However, the mission and methods of Operation Gladio went far beyond merely preparing for a potential Soviet occupation. It became deeply entangled in covert activities, including political manipulation, propaganda, and acts of terrorism, all aimed at influencing the political landscape of Europe. The operation's existence was only confirmed in 1990, leading to a wave of political scandals and inquiries across Europe.

The origins of Operation Gladio can be traced back to the early days of the Cold War when Western European countries, backed by the United States, feared the spread of communism across the continent. To counteract this perceived threat, NATO and the CIA initiated a series of secret stay-behind armies, composed of selected individuals trained in guerrilla warfare, sabotage, and covert operations. These operatives were tasked with organizing resistance movements and conducting intelligence activities in the event of a Soviet invasion. Italy was a focal point of this network, and Gladio was the codename for the Italian arm of the operation.

The official purpose of Operation Gladio was to ensure that Western European countries could continue to resist Soviet forces even if their governments were overthrown. However, as details of the operation began to surface, it became evident that Gladio's activities were not limited to defending against an invasion. Instead, these stay-behind armies were used to influence domestic politics in Western

European nations, often through violent and undemocratic means. In Italy, where the Communist Party was particularly strong, Gladio operatives engaged in a strategy of tension, which sought to create an atmosphere of fear and instability that could be exploited to sway public opinion and justify authoritarian measures.

One of the most controversial aspects of Operation Gladio was its alleged involvement in terrorist attacks and false flag operations. These acts of violence were intended to be blamed on left-wing groups, particularly communist organizations, thereby discrediting them in the eyes of the public and bolstering support for more conservative or authoritarian governments. The most infamous of these incidents was the 1980 bombing of the Bologna railway station, which killed eighty-five people and injured over two hundred. Initially blamed on left-wing extremists, it was later revealed that right-wing militants with ties to Gladio and other stay-behind networks were responsible for the attack. This and other similar incidents have led to widespread speculation that Gladio was not merely a defensive operation but was actively involved in manipulating public sentiment and suppressing political opposition.

Operation Gladio's influence extended beyond Italy to several other European countries, including Belgium, France, Germany, Greece, and Türkiye. In Belgium, for example, the existence of a stay-behind army was linked to a series of violent incidents in the 1980s known as the Brabant massacres, in which heavily armed shooters attacked supermarkets and other public places, killing twenty-eight people. These attacks, which were never fully solved, have been speculatively connected to Gladio operatives seeking to create chaos and fear to destabilize the country and shift the political climate to the right.

In Greece, the stay-behind network was implicated in the 1967 military coup that overthrew the democratic government and established a military junta that ruled the country for seven years.

The Greek branch of Gladio was alleged to have provided support to the coup plotters, who feared that the growing influence of left-wing political movements might lead Greece to abandon its alignment with the West. Similarly, in Türkiye, Gladio operatives were linked to the so-called "Deep State," a shadowy network within the government, military, and intelligence services that orchestrated political violence, assassinations, and coups to maintain control over the country and suppress perceived threats from leftist groups.

As more information about Operation Gladio began to emerge in the late 20th century, it sparked widespread outrage and calls for accountability across Europe. The revelations began in Italy in 1990 when then-Prime Minister Giulio Andreotti publicly acknowledged the existence of Gladio, claiming it was a necessary measure against the Soviet threat. However, this admission led to investigations that uncovered a far more sinister role for the stay-behind networks, particularly in relation to domestic terrorism and political manipulation. Parliamentary inquiries were launched in Italy, Belgium, and Switzerland, among other countries, to investigate the extent of Gladio's activities and the involvement of state officials in covert operations that targeted their own citizens.

The European Parliament itself issued a resolution condemning Gladio in 1990, calling for a full investigation into the network's activities and demanding that all information related to the operation be declassified and made public. Despite these efforts, much of the information surrounding Gladio remains shrouded in secrecy, with many of the key details either classified or obscured by conflicting accounts. This lack of transparency has fueled numerous conspiracy theories and debates over the true extent of Gladio's operations and its impact on European politics.

The legacy of Operation Gladio is one of deep distrust and suspicion toward the government institutions involved in these clandestine activities. The operation has been cited as an example of the lengths to which states will go to maintain control and influence, even at the cost of democratic principles and human lives. The strategic use of fear, violence, and misinformation to manipulate political outcomes has had lasting effects on the political landscape of several European countries, leading to a lingering sense of unease about the true nature of state power and the potential for similar operations to be conducted in the future.

The controversy surrounding Operation Gladio has also had a significant impact on public perception of NATO and the CIA, both of which were heavily involved in the creation and operation of the stay-behind networks. The revelations about Gladio have contributed to a broader critique of Western intelligence agencies and their role in covert operations that undermine democratic processes and violate human rights. In the years since the operation was exposed, there have been numerous calls for greater oversight and accountability for intelligence activities, both within Europe and in other parts of the world where similar operations may have been conducted.

In conclusion, Operation Gladio was a clandestine NATO operation that, while initially conceived as a defensive measure against a potential Soviet invasion, evolved into a far more insidious campaign of political manipulation and violence. Through its involvement in terrorist attacks, false flag operations, and political interference, Gladio played a significant role in shaping the political landscape of post-war Europe, often at the expense of democratic principles and human lives. The operation's exposure in the 1990s led to widespread political scandal, calls for accountability, and a reevaluation of the role of intelligence agencies in democratic societies. Despite the efforts to uncover the full extent of Gladio's activities, much about the operation remains hidden, leaving many questions unanswered and contributing to ongoing debates about the true nature of state power and the ethics of covert operations.

COINTELPRO and Operation Gladio, though distinct in their specific contexts, share a strong correlation in their objectives, tactics, and the broader Cold War-era strategies they were part of. Both programs were deeply rooted in anti-communist sentiments and sought to suppress political dissent and maintain control over what were perceived as subversive threats. COINTELPRO, a domestic U.S. operation, targeted groups such as civil rights organizations, leftist movements, and activists who were seen as sympathetic to communism or as threats to national security. In contrast, Operation Gladio was an international effort primarily based in Europe, aimed at preventing the spread of communism, particularly in countries where leftist parties were gaining influence.

The methods employed by COINTELPRO and Operation Gladio bear striking comparisons particularly in their reliance on surveillance, infiltration, and psychological warfare. COINTELPRO agents infiltrated domestic organizations to gather intelligence, create internal divisions, and disrupt activities. Similarly, Gladio operatives were embedded within European resistance movements and other organizations, working clandestinely to undermine communist influence. Both programs made extensive use of psychological operations, with COINTELPRO using disinformation, forged documents, and anonymous letters to create mistrust and paranoia within targeted groups. Operation Gladio also engaged in psychological tactics, spreading fear and disinformation to destabilize political environments and justify anti-communist measures. Additionally, Operation Gladio is explicitly linked to false-flag operations, where terrorist acts were staged and blamed on left-wing groups to discredit them, a tactic not directly associated with COINTELPRO but aligned with its manipulative strategies.

These programs were part of a larger pattern of Cold War-era covert operations conducted by the U.S. and its allies, designed to counter threats from the Soviet Union and its allies, as well as from domestic and international movements challenging capitalist and Western democratic norms. Both COINTELPRO and Operation Gladio operated in secrecy, often without oversight or accountability, leading to public outcry and significant questions about the abuse of government power when they were eventually exposed. The legacy of these programs has contributed to a deep mistrust of government, particularly in how it deals with dissent and opposition, and has influenced modern statecraft, especially in counterterrorism, surveillance, and information warfare. The ongoing relevance of the tactics and strategies employed by COINTELPRO and Operation Gladio can be seen in contemporary concerns about government overreach, civil liberties, and the use of covert operations to control political outcomes. Despite their differences in focus—one domestic and the other international—COINTELPRO and Operation Gladio are linked by their shared goals of suppressing dissent and maintaining state control during a period of intense geopolitical tension.

On November 22, 1990, the European Parliament passed a resolution on Operation

Gladio. Joint resolution replacing B3-2021, 2058, 2068, 2087/90 reads as follows:

A. Having regard to the revelation by several European governments of the existence for

40 years of a clandestine parallel intelligence and armed operations organization in

several member states of the community,

B. whereas for over 40 years this organization has escaped all democratic controls and

has been run by the secret services of the states concerned in collaboration with NATO,

C. fearing the danger that such clandestine network may have interfered illegally in the

internal political affairs of Member States or may still do so,

D. where in certain Member States military secret services (or uncontrolled branches

thereof) engaged in serious cases of terrorism and crime as evidenced by various

judicial inquiries.

E. whereas these organizations operated and continue to operate completely outside the

law since they are not subject to any parliamentary control and frequently those holding

the highest government and constitutional posts are kept in the dark as to these matters,

F. whereas the various "Gladio" organizations have at their disposal independent arsenals

and military resources which give them an unknown strike potential, thereby jeopardizing

the democratic structures of the countries in which they are operating or have been

operating,

G. concerned at the existence of decision-making and operational bodies which

are not subject to any form of democratic control and are of a completely clandestine

nature at a time when greater Community cooperation in the field of security is a

constant subject of discussion.

1. Condemns the clandestine creation of manipulative and operational networks and calls

for full investigation into the nature, structure, aims and all other aspects of the

clandestine organizations or any splinter group, their use of illegal interference in the international political affairs of the countries concerned the problem of terrorism in

Europe and the possible collusion of the secret services of Member States or third

countries.

2. Protests vigorously at the assumption by certain US military personnel at SHAPE and in

NATO of the right to encourage the establishment in Europe of a clandestine intelligence

and operation network.

3. Calls on the governments of the Member States to dismantle all clandestine military

and paramilitary networks.

4. Calls on the judiciaries of countries in which the presence of such military organizations

has been ascertained to elucidate fully their composition and modus operandi and to

clarify any action they may have taken to destabilize the democratic structure of the

Member states.

5. Request all the Member States to take the necessary measures, if necessary, by

establishing parliamentary committee of inquiry, to draw up a complete list of

organizations active in this field, and at the same time monitor their links with the

respective state intelligence services and their links, if any, with terrorists' action groups

and/or other illegal practices.

6. Calls on the Council of Ministers to provide full information on the activities of these

secret intelligence and operational services.

7. Calls on its competent committee to consider holding a hearing to clarify the

role and impact of the "Gladio" organization and any similar bodies.

8. Instructs its President to forward this resolution to the Commission, the Council, the

Secretary-General of NATO, the governments of the Member States and the United States

Government."

Operation Gladio's current impact is felt through its lasting legacy on European politics, public trust in government, and the ongoing concerns about covert operations and state-sponsored manipulation. Although Gladio was officially dismantled in the early 1990s, its effects continue to influence both the political landscape and public discourse in several ways:

1. Erosion of Public Trust: The revelations about Gladio have contributed to a deep mistrust of government institutions, particularly intelligence agencies and military operations. Many citizens, especially in countries where Gladio was active, remain skeptical about the transparency and accountability of their governments. This distrust is exacerbated by fears that similar operations might still be ongoing under different guises, potentially targeting new perceived threats.

2. Political Instability: The memory of Gladio and its tactics continues to shape political narratives, particularly in Southern and Eastern Europe. In Italy, for instance, the "strategy of tension" employed by Gladio, which involved acts of terrorism to create fear and justify authoritarian measures, is often cited in discussions about current political strategies. The idea that governments might use fear to manipulate public opinion and maintain control remains a potent concern, especially in times of crisis.

3. Rise of Conspiracy Theories: Gladio has become a central theme in numerous conspiracy theories that suggest ongoing covert

operations by state or international actors. These theories often draw parallels between Gladio and modern-day events, such as false flag operations, political assassinations, or unexplained terrorist attacks. While not always based on solid evidence, these theories reflect a broader concern about the secretive nature of government operations and their potential to undermine democracy.

4. Increased Scrutiny of Intelligence Agencies: The exposure of Gladio has led to greater scrutiny of intelligence agencies, both in Europe and globally. There is a heightened awareness of the potential for abuse of power within these agencies, leading to calls for increased oversight and transparency. Legislative bodies and civil society organizations have pushed for more rigorous checks on intelligence activities to prevent the recurrence of operations like Gladio.

5. Influence on Populist Movements: The legacy of Gladio has been invoked by populist movements across Europe, which often position themselves as defenders of the people against corrupt elites and shadowy state operations. These movements use the history of Gladio to argue that established political parties and institutions cannot be trusted, thereby fueling anti-establishment sentiments, and contributing to the rise of populism.

6. Historical Re-examinations: The history of Gladio has prompted ongoing re-examinations of past political events, particularly unsolved crimes, terrorist attacks, and coups in Europe during the Cold War. Historians, journalists, and independent investigators continue to explore the possibility that Gladio or similar operations engaged in these events, seeking to uncover the truth and provide justice for victims.

7. Impact on EU Security Policies: Within the European Union, the legacy of Gladio has influenced discussions on security policies and the balance between national security and civil liberties. The EU has had to grapple with the challenges of ensuring security without

repeating the mistakes of the past, where security concerns were used to justify undemocratic practices.

In summary, the current impact of Operation Gladio is reflected in the lingering mistrust of government, the shaping of political discourse, and ongoing concerns about the use of covert operations to influence domestic and international affairs. Gladio's legacy continues to serve as a cautionary tale about the dangers of unchecked state power and the importance of transparency and accountability in preserving democratic values.

OTHER TACTICS (as compiled by Dr. Rauni Kilde)

There are other tactics which are not strictly part of the categories discussed so far:

-IMPORTANT: Community-based agents (CBAs) are strictly forbidden from adding anyone

to the list of targets. Target selection is done by senior Control Center (CC) staff or higher

levels.

-Punishment of people who side with and help the target. Friends, family members, and

citizens who do not place a high value on community sometimes help targets. In these

extremely specific cases, CC-authorized punishment in the form of individual acts against them

is appropriate. The system can arrange for these target sympathizers to be found guilty of

crimes, or liable for civil actions, for example. This is important for maintenance of the

system.

-Target bank accounts can be disrupted in ways which do not give the target cause to

involve law enforcement. Examples: target protection can be changed to "youth account,"

or, an overdraft protection feature can be disabled, or simply steal money from the

account. It is called action of "international banking ring" and usually at first the sums are

around 50 – one hundred dollars which are taken when the target pays small bills.

-Money is never transferred to the journal subscription or membership in a certain club

like "opposition to government surveillance." Money simply "disappears" from the bank

with help of cooperating employers. I have experienced the myself several times. Bank

accounts are "hacked" for the payment and a new bill arrives for the already paid bill by

the target, and the receipt of payment is stolen. There is cooperation with military

intelligence, Stay behind, NATO, and foreign intelligence agencies also against their own

population. (This is the) so-called secret silent war going on in all secrecy.

Appendix 4: From Total Individual Control Technology by Omnisense

Organized Stalking/Electronic Harassment. The New Hi-Tech Generation of COINTELPRO

In a Nutshell: Government sources are using directed energy weapons and artificial

intelligence to terrorize, threaten, intimidate, discredit, silence, torture, and murder

dissidents. In addition, security contractors (among others) are being hired as military

thugs to gang stalk targets [19].

Zerzetsen: "Inflicting as much pain and suffering as possible without leaving any

marks.[20]" Directed energy weapon programs revolutionized this...

Counter-proliferation programs are intended to subvert the potentials of a target while punishing them with psycho-sadist techniques. The perversions of cointelpro are notable.

The murderous and sadistic ethos of government counter-proliferation programs echoes

that of the Nazis and this perpetrator network of war criminals are committing sickening

acts upon the global population.

Modern Day COINTELPRO
Objectives:

These are counter-proliferation centered programs intended to subvert all progress

To discredit the target / To character assassinate / To slander the target

To taint the target's image / To misrepresent the target

To suppress the target's monetary success

To suppress the target's good character qualities or people's awareness of positive

aspects of the target

To arrange a partner for the target or mind control the partner of the target

To destroy relationships of the target

To co-opt the target's manifestation

To turn the target into controlled opposition (In terms of beliefs & actions)

To incriminate the target

To round down the target's output and audience – To marginalize the target

To eliminate connections & networking ability

To suppress the target's personality

Sanitization of pleasure, emotions, and individuality

To punish the target / To torture the target

To destroy the target's life

To stop a target from procreating / Ending a target's bloodline (Eugenics)

To suicide the target / To covertly assassinate the target

To cover up the targeting operation

"If they see too much power and originality coming out of someone, they either use it

and siphon it or they undermine it to neutralize it." ~Ahmad Enani (TI)

COINTELPRO 2.0 Methodology:

Covert remote influencing technology suite

COINTELPRO 2.0: Thought surveillance neural AI net for psyche profiling

COINTELPRO 2.0: Directed energy weapon mind control network for counter-proliferation

targeting

Ai based retro-causation; Extensive international neural monitoring programs can

calculate a target's potentials before the target is aware of them

Gang stalking / Organized Stalking

Trauma based mind control – No touch torture

Character assassination / Slander via proxies

Technological illusions (PSYOPS) / misdirection

Electromagnetic mind control aimed at discrediting the target

Mind control of people who provide opportunities for the target

Use of family against the target (e.g., Mind control of family)

Use of pharmaceutical drugs against a target

To orchestrate the detaining of the target in a psyche ward

v2k to get a target diagnosed as a "paranoid schizophrenic"

Exaggerated, warped and untrue slander about the target is proliferated

Technology playing devil's advocate via implanted thoughts to get a target in trouble

Agenda to incriminate the target (Advice for COINTELPRO targets: Stay lawful)

Use of ego against a target

Weaponized mind control against a target

Coercing of a target into appearing overly paranoid (e.g., An objective of stalking)

Specific technological control of a target's body language or vocal tone (e.g., To generate

mistrust)

Total individual control technology is used as a tactic to take away a citizen's rights

through faulty mental illness diagnoses [21]

Outlandish black project technology experiences intended to discredit when spoken

Use of electronic control grid to mind control misfortunes for a target

Synthetic social phobias ~ Synthetic social anxiety (e.g., public speaker related

suppression)

Suppression of whatever platform the target is talented in (e.g., Music production,

software design)

To dehumanize a target via electromagnetic neuroscience

Severe targets are sanitized of pleasure, emotions, and personality

Synthetic suicide programming

Technologically enabled serial killers with a taste for revolutionaries & activists

Electronic Targeting Holocaust

"While all these traditional tactics have proven fruitful throughout time without waning

effectiveness, the agencies involved in extreme cover-ups prefer another tactic that

seems to have withstood the test of time too. That is labeling someone "paranoid

schizophrenic" or mentally ill. Once that label has been attached to someone, all testimony will be disbelieved. The military has employed this tactic since the sixty's to get

rebellious soldiers and others locked up in mental hospitals. But since the weapons

testing of neurological disruptor technology has begun on the general population

beginning in the early sixty's and then stepped up to full throttle in 1976, the scope of what

is considered mentally ill had to be reprogrammed into a broader definition for the

general population." ~Department of Defense Whistleblower: From the Out-of-Print Book

– The Matrix Deciphered

"My name is Dr. John Hall, I am a medical Doctor from Texas. As a physician, relative to

some of what you hear today, in the community we see an alarming rate of

complaints of use of electromagnetic weapons, microwave auditory effect, silent sound

spectrum, EEG cloning, ... Which has taken the lab out of the laboratory and into the

home, most of these from the research that we have reviewed can be done remotely. It

seems to be more weapons research than medical research. I have personally corresponded

with upwards of 1,500 victims all complaining of identical complaints from every state in

the nation. Of being exposed to electromagnetic radiation. Non-ionizing radiation. For the

use of cognitive control or behavior control...." ~Anesthesiologist Dr. John Hall Speaking

to the Presidential Bioethics Commission

"I am also targeted, and this is my story. My name is Sandra Fields. I am an architect,

recipient of Who's Who of Women in America achievement award and have run a

successful business for over 28 years. My life and livelihood have been compromised for

the last 11 years by being attacked by electromagnetic radiation torture, and by

organized stalking... Thousands of Americans are currently suffering from chemical,

electromagnetic, psychological, and physical torture with no government relief or laws.

Our service members, prisoners, and thousands of unknowing innocent civilians are currently

being lamed, tormented, and tortured as a result of military research, medical research,

pharmaceutical research, physiological and psychological studies that have virtually

destroyed participants' sanity, physical well-being, reputation, and privacy." ~Targeted

Individual Sandra Fields, Speaking to Obama's Presidential Bioethics Committee

"What the governments found, was that you could induce by changing the pulse

frequency like morse code of the microwaves going into the brain and interfering with

the brain, by specializing on the pulse frequency you could induce psychiatric illnesses to

the point where a psychiatrist could not tell whether it is a genuine psychiatric illness or an

induced psychiatric illness. So, what you can do theoretically, is you can target an individual's brain, they may have auditory hallucinations where they hear things, which is

quite common with microwaves. Or show signs of schizophrenia, for instance 6.6

pulses a second can induce severe sexual aggression in men. ... Technically what you

could do is have someone committed to a psychiatric hospital or a jail for a crime, just by

somebody saying that they had a psychiatric problem whereby they did not."

~Ex-British Royal Navy Scientist Dr. Barrie Trower

"They can cause insanity, and it was an experiment. One of the experiments was to take

an ordinary sane person, cause insanity, and have a psychiatrist who was unknown to

Everybody diagnoses schizophrenia, or paranoia or a psychiatric illness. That was a

successful outcome. And the person would spend the rest of their life in an asylum in

misery, but to the government scientists that was a success." ~Ex-Black Project Scientist

Dr. Barrie Trower

"The war against satellite terrorism is not just the USA. This is a global issue! I am in tropical

Queensland Australia and get battered daily." ~Targeted Individual Amanda Emily Reed

MKULTRA Cover Stories

This technology has interacted with quite a large amount of people, however it is almost

always misidentified as other sources [8].

Directed Energy Weapon Cover Stories:

Mental illness as an electronic harassment cover story

End game technology packaged under persuasive "spiritual warfare" illusions

Directed energy interaction packaged as the supernatural

Government technology under a cosmic being facade

Religious themed illusions / Using religion mythology as a means for cover stories

Extraterrestrial contact as a psychological operation cover story

Ghosts as a cover story – AI orchestrated phantom illusions

End game technology as a sorcery cover story

End game technology as the real source behind effective voodoo

Witchcraft as a directed energy cover story

Black project science under a black magic cover story

Directed energy attacks deceptively packaged as physiological ailments

Synthetic signals in the brain from implants framed as physiological ailments

"Psychic Attack" as a directed energy attack cover story

"Spiritual Attack" as a directed energy attack cover story

New Age cover stories (e.g., Disembodied spirit illusions)

Old age mythological gods used as a cover story

Human based electronic harassment with aliens packaged as the perpetrator

Scientology methods as a cover story for technological remote influence

Exotic neurobody illusions (e.g., Chakra, entity attachments, ethereal implants)

Inter dimensional being interaction as an electronic targeting cover story

Exploitation of illusory explanations to conceal directed energy crimes

"People who have already assimilated the cover stories are often not ready to hear the truth." ~Omnisense

Beings Impersonated:

Neighbors (Targeted Individual v2k)

Black Ops Agents (Targeted Individual v2k)

Family (Targeted Individual v2k)

Deceased Loved Ones / Deceased Relatives / Deceased Pets (PsyOps v2k)

Demons (Mind Control Cover Story)

Jinn (Cover Stories)

Archons (Cover Stories)

Inter Dimensional Beings (New Age PsyOps)

Extraterrestrials (Cosmic Being Impersonation Programs / Ufology Bastardization)

Entity Attachments (New Age PsyOps)

Shadow Beings (e.g., To Cause Fear from an Obscure Source)

Archangels (To Impersonate a Higher Authority)

Lucifer (To Persuade into Evil)

Satan (Satanist v2k)

RA (New Age PsyOps)

Spirits (Spiritual Warfare Illusions)

Ghosts – Phantoms (Directed Energy Trickery)

Faeries (Rehashed Old Age Cover Stories)

Higher Self (Mind Control Cover Story)

Panpsychism Based Impersonations (e.g., Gaia aka Mother Earth Speaking to People)

Saints & Mother Mary (Religious Impersonations)

Holy Spirit (Psychological Direction Method / Sleeper Assassin Method)

Ascended Masters (Impersonation of a Higher Power)

Jesus (Any Vector of Vulnerability is Exploited)

Persons of Note (e.g., To get a Target to Murder them, To Psychologically Direct)

Any Mythological God of the Past (These can be cool)

God / Allah / Yahweh / Jehovah (Impersonation of the Highest Power)

Done via Electronic Telepathy Contact (Voice to Skull – v2k)

"Directed energy weapons operate invisibly while the inducible mental limits of directed

energy weapons are the limits of consciousness itself, this makes for an incredibly potent

environment for illusions of all types." ~Omnisense

NeuroWeaponry & Artificial Intelligence Quotes

"The point of the program is to have maximum psychological effect and leave the

minimal amount of evidence.[22]" ~Anonymous Targeting Program Insider

"In 1985 CNN did a special report on radio frequency weapons. They hired an engineer

who built an "RF Mind Interference" machine based on Soviet schematics. The machine

successfully transmitted images into a CNN reporter's mind. The stunned engineer said

that, given three weeks' time, he could scale up the machine to use on a whole town,

causing them to do things against their better judgement, see and hear things that

were not there, etc. The pentagon said it was too sensitive a subject to comment on.

Remember, these effects were achieved by civilians over 30 years ago! One can speculate

that they have made great advances in the past decades.[8]" ~Targeted Individual Jim Hastings

Disinformation Campaigns

Disinformation campaigns, where false or misleading information is deliberately spread to influence public opinion or create confusion, have been prominent in recent years. Here are notable examples:

Russian Interference in the 2016 U.S. Presidential Election:

Social Media Manipulation: Russian operatives, particularly through the Internet Research Agency (IRA), created fake social media accounts and pages to spread divisive content, fake news stories, and conspiracy theories. This included promoting both pro-Trump and anti-Clinton narratives to polarize voters and sow discord.

Hack-and-Dump Operations: Russian intelligence agencies hacked emails from the Democratic National Committee (DNC) and John Podesta, then leaked these materials through WikiLeaks to damage Hillary Clinton's campaign and influence the election outcome.

COVID-19 Misinformation:

Virus Origins and Treatments: During the COVID-19 pandemic, disinformation spread widely about the virus's origins, claiming it was artificially created or linked to conspiracy theories about bioweapons. False cures and treatments, such as unproven drugs or remedies, were promoted, contributing to public confusion and health risks.

Vaccine Misinformation: Campaigns spread false claims about COVID-19 vaccines, including that they were part of a plot for population control or that they contained harmful ingredients. This misinformation has fueled vaccine hesitancy and impacted public health efforts.

QAnon Conspiracy Theory:

Child Trafficking and Secret Cabals: The QAnon movement spread disinformation about a secret cabal of pedophiles controlling the world, with prominent politicians and celebrities allegedly involved. This baseless conspiracy theory gained significant traction online, influencing political discourse and leading to real-world consequences, including violence and harassment.

Chinese Disinformation Campaigns:

Protests and Political Unrest: China has been accused of spreading disinformation about political protests, such as those in Hong Kong and Taiwan. Fake social media accounts and state-controlled media outlets have disseminated misleading information to discredit protesters and influence international opinion.

The "Pizzagate" Conspiracy:

Fake Child Abuse Ring: The "Pizzagate" conspiracy falsely claimed that a Washington, D.C., pizzeria was the center of a child sex trafficking ring involving high-profile political figures. This disinformation led to real-world consequences, including threats and a shooting incident at the pizzeria.

Brexit Referendum Disinformation:

Fake News and Misleading Claims: During the 2016 Brexit referendum, various disinformation tactics were employed, including the spread of false claims about the economic impacts of leaving the European Union and misleading advertisements about immigration. These tactics influenced voter opinions and the referendum outcome.

Syria Conflict Propaganda:

Chemical Weapons Allegations: In the Syrian Civil War, conflicting claims and propaganda about chemical weapons attacks were disseminated by various parties. Disinformation about who was responsible for attacks and their scale was used to influence international opinion and justify military actions.

Iranian Disinformation Campaigns:

Influencing U.S. Politics: Iran has been involved in disinformation campaigns aimed at influencing U.S. politics, including spreading false narratives and inflammatory content on social media to create political divisions and undermine confidence in the electoral process.

These examples illustrate how disinformation campaigns can affect political processes, public health, and social cohesion by spreading false or misleading information to achieve specific goals.

Current disinformation campaigns 2020-present

Here is a comprehensive list of disputed statements and claims by the Biden administration, including the entities involved and the fact-checking information:

1. *COVID-19 Vaccines and Effectiveness*

Claim: The vaccines are highly effective in preventing COVID-19 and severe illness.

Entity: Biden Administration

Example: Statements suggesting near-complete immunity from vaccines.

Fact-Checking: Fact-checkers, such as PolitiFact and FactCheck.org, confirmed high effectiveness but noted breakthrough infections and varying effectiveness over time.

2. *Inflation and Economic Policies*

Claim: The American Rescue Plan had negligible impact on inflation.

Entity: Biden Administration

Example: Claims about the stimulus package's minimal effect on inflation.

Fact-Checking: PolitiFact and FactCheck.org highlighted the debate, noting both global and domestic factors contribute to inflation.

3. *Border and Immigration Policies*

Claim: Conditions at the border have improved and the administration has managed the migrant crisis effectively.

Entity: Biden Administration

Example: Claims of improved border conditions and effective crisis management.

Fact-Checking: Reuters and PolitiFact reported ongoing challenges and significant issues contradicting the administration's optimistic portrayal.

4. *Afghanistan Withdrawal*

Claim: The withdrawal from Afghanistan was well-planned and executed.

Entity: Biden Administration

Example: Claims about a successful and orderly evacuation.

Fact-Checking: Reports from various outlets, including CNN and The New York Times, revealed chaos and significant issues during the withdrawal.

5. *Gas Prices and Energy Policies*

Claim: Rising gas prices are primarily due to global factors, not domestic policies.

Entity: Biden Administration

Example: Claims that domestic energy policies had minimal impact on gas prices.

Fact-Checking: The Washington Post Fact Checker and FactCheck.org noted that while global factors are significant, domestic policies also influence energy prices.

6. *Student Loan Forgiveness*

Claim: The student loan forgiveness plan is legally sound and will significantly benefit borrowers.

Entity: Biden Administration

Example: Claims about the legality and impact of the forgiveness program.

Fact-Checking: FactCheck.org and PolitiFact pointed out potential legal challenges and debated the program's actual impact.

7. *Ukraine and U.S. Support*

Claim: U.S. support for Ukraine has been effective and substantial.

Entity: Biden Administration

Example: Claims about the extent and impact of military and financial aid.

Fact-Checking: FactCheck.org and Reuters provided context on the complexities of measuring the effectiveness of U.S. support.

8. *Supply Chain and Inflation*

Claim: The administration has effectively addressed supply chain issues and inflation.

Entity: Biden Administration

Example: Statements about successful management of supply chain disruptions.

Fact-Checking: Fact-checkers like PolitiFact highlighted ongoing issues and the complex relationship between administration policies and inflation.

9. *COVID-19 Vaccination Mandates*

Claim: Vaccination mandates will effectively increase vaccination rates and ensure public safety.

Entity: Biden Administration

Example: Claims about the effectiveness of mandates in improving public health.

Fact-Checking: FactCheck.org and other sources noted legal and practical challenges to mandates and mixed results in increasing vaccination rates.

10. *Climate Change Policies*

Claim: The administration's climate policies will lead to significant environmental improvements.

Entity: Biden Administration

Example: Claims about the positive effects of climate policies.

Fact-Checking: PolitiFact and FactCheck.org provided context on the long-term nature of climate policy impacts and the complexities involved.

11. *Social Security and Medicare*

Claim: The administration's policies will protect and expand Social Security and Medicare benefits.

Entity: Biden Administration

Example: Claims about enhancing benefits and addressing financial challenges.

Fact-Checking: FactCheck.org and other sources highlighted the complexities and challenges of reforming Social Security and Medicare.

12. *Economic Growth and Job Creation*

Claim: The administration's policies have significantly boosted economic growth and job creation.

Entity: Biden Administration

Example: Claims about the positive impact of policies on employment and growth.

Fact-Checking: FactCheck.org and PolitiFact reviewed the claims, noting job creation while recognizing the influence of multiple factors on economic growth.

13. *Immigration Enforcement*

Claim: The administration's approach to immigration enforcement is both humane and effective.

Entity: Biden Administration

Example: Claims about balanced and effective immigration policies.

Fact-Checking: Fact-checkers noted ongoing issues and debates about the effectiveness and humanity of the administration's immigration enforcement strategies.

14. *Voting Rights Legislation*

Claim: Voting rights legislation is essential for protecting democracy and preventing voter suppression.

Entity: Biden Administration

Example: Claims about the necessity and impact of voting rights reforms.

Fact-Checking: FactCheck.org and PolitiFact examined the claims, providing context on the complexities of voting rights issues and legislative impacts.

15. *Racial Equity and Social Justice*

Claim: The administration has made significant progress in advancing racial equity and social justice.

Entity: Biden Administration

Example: Claims about achievements in racial equity and social justice.

Fact-Checking: Fact-checkers noted ongoing debates and challenges in measuring and achieving progress in these areas.

These examples cover a range of claims made by the Biden administration, each scrutinized by fact-checking organizations to provide accurate context and address any discrepancies.

False Flag Operations

A false flag operation is a covert activity designed to deceive by making it appear as though an action or incident was carried out by a different entity than the actual perpetrators. This tactic is employed to mislead, manipulate, or achieve specific strategic, political, or tactical objectives. The primary goal of *a false flag operation is to create the illusion that an attack or event was the work of an opposing or unrelated group.* This deception is often executed through various means, including disguising the identity of the actors, using misleading symbols, or staging events to implicate the intended target.

The motives behind false flag operations can be diverse. They may include provoking conflict by inciting retaliatory actions against a targeted group or nation, undermining political opponents by attributing nefarious activities to them, or manipulating public opinion to sway support for controversial policies or actions. For instance, during the Cold War, Operation Gladio involved NATO and associated intelligence services orchestrating covert operations, some of which included false flag attacks. These attacks were staged to appear as if they were carried out by leftist or communist groups, thereby justifying anti-communist measures and discrediting political adversaries.

Historical examples illustrate the use of false flag operations. The Reichstag fire in 1933, which destroyed the German parliament building, was manipulated by the Nazi Party to blame communist agitators. This event facilitated a crackdown on political opponents and helped Adolf Hitler consolidate power. Similarly, the Gulf of Tonkin incident in 1964 involved exaggerated or misrepresented claims of attacks on U.S. naval vessels by North Vietnamese forces. This incident was used to justify increased U.S. military involvement in Vietnam, demonstrating how false flag operations can shape public opinion and influence political decisions.

False flag operations typically involve staging events, using disguises and symbols, and manipulating evidence. Perpetrators may fabricate or stage incidents to create a desired narrative, employ disguises or fake symbols to mislead observers, and alter or plant evidence to support the false narrative. These tactics are designed to make it appear as though the targeted entity was responsible for the actions or events in question.

One such action that received very little press coverage was the case of Davin Daniel Meyer In 2020, there were allegations and reports involving an FBI agent accused of attempting to groom a mentally challenged youth to become a mass shooter. The case in question involved an undercover FBI agent, Richard Trask, who was allegedly involved in a controversial entrapment operation. There are other cases involving youth and the FBI targeting young and mentally challenged individuals to become shooters, such as Mateo Ventura, Humzah

Mashkoor, Mahin Khan, and Sami Osmakac. With each subsequent mass shooting, usually targeting schools and places where young adults gather, and the direct push for gun control legislation that slowly is eroding the ability for the United States citizens to bear arms, it has become apparent to a grown number of people that the manufactured violence by the FBI is politically motivated and uses fearmongering to manipulate the populace into giving up its rights and further place themselves in a vulnerable position where a dictatorial government can take over with ease.

The implications of false flag operations are significant, affecting political and social dynamics. They can lead to unjust wars, escalate conflicts, and create long-term animosity between groups or nations. The manipulation of public opinion through such operations can undermine trust in institutions and media. Ethically, false flag operations raise serious concerns as they involve deception, manipulation, and sometimes violence, resulting in harm to innocent parties. The legacy of false flag operations contributes to a broader understanding of covert activities and their impact on global affairs, shedding light on the complex interplay of politics, deception, and power.

incidents considered potential false flag operations

Here is a broad list of incidents considered potential false flag operations, including the policies or social changes that resulted:

FBI's 2016 Plot Against the Muslim Community

Incident: FBI arrests of four men allegedly plotting an attack on a mosque and a Jewish community center.

Criteria for False Flag Allegation:

Informant Involvement: Concerns about informants influencing the plot.

Manipulation Concerns: Claims of exaggeration to justify broader actions.

Resulting Policy/Social Change:

Increased Surveillance: Enhanced surveillance and monitoring of Muslim communities.

Debate on Informant Tactics: Discussions about the ethics of informant use in counterterrorism.

2021 U.S. Capitol Riot and Conspiracy Theories

Incident: Attack on the U.S. Capitol by Trump supporters on January 6, 2021.

Criteria for False Flag Allegation:

Unverified Claims: Speculations about orchestrated attacks to discredit Trump supporters.

Lack of Evidence: Confirmed as an act by domestic extremists.

Resulting Policy/Social Change:

Increased Security Measures: Enhanced security protocols at the Capitol and other federal buildings.

Legislative Actions: Legislative proposals to address domestic extremism and improve security.

The FBI's 2020 kidnapping plot against Michigan Governor Gretchen Whitmer has been scrutinized by some observers as a potential false flag operation. Here's an examination of the incident through the lens of false flag criteria:

In October 2020, the FBI announced the arrest of 13 individuals who were allegedly involved in a plot to kidnap Michigan Governor Gretchen Whitmer. The plot was reportedly motivated by the group's opposition to Whitmer's strict COVID-19 lockdown measures. The FBI's investigation led to the arrest of the individuals, who were charged with conspiracy and other related offenses. According to the FBI, the group intended to capture and potentially harm the governor as part of a broader anti-government agenda.

Criteria for False Flag Allegation

Political Timing: The timing of the FBI's announcement of the plot was significant, coming just weeks before the 2020 U.S. presidential election. The revelation of the plot against a high-profile political figure like Governor Whitmer had the potential to influence public perception of political extremism and domestic terrorism. Critics argued that the timing was strategically advantageous for highlighting the threat of right-wing extremism in the lead-up to the election, thereby shaping political narratives and responses.

Individual Motives: The alleged plotters were purportedly motivated by their opposition to Governor Whitmer's lockdown measures and their broader anti-government stance. However, some critics suggested that the FBI's handling of the case might have served ulterior motives. There were claims that FBI informants and undercover agents played a substantial role in the planning and execution of the plot, raising questions about the extent to which the FBI might have influenced or facilitated the alleged conspiracy. This raised concerns about whether the operation was, in part, a maneuver to create a politically advantageous narrative.

Resulting Policy: The fallout from the FBI's announcement contributed to increased scrutiny of right-wing extremism and domestic terrorism in the U.S. The case was used to underscore the threats posed by radical anti-government groups and to advocate for more stringent counter-terrorism measures. It influenced policy discussions around domestic security and the monitoring of extremist groups, contributing to a broader narrative about the dangers of political violence and extremism. The case also had implications for public perceptions of the FBI's role in counter-terrorism and its methods of investigation.

Analysis

The FBI's 2020 kidnapping plot against Governor Whitmer has been viewed by some as potentially fitting the criteria for a false flag operation, particularly concerning political timing and the role of law enforcement in the plot. The strategic timing of the announcement, coupled with the involvement of informants and undercover agents, has fueled speculation about the possibility of the operation being used to advance specific political or policy agendas. Critics argue that the case's high-profile nature and its impact on public discourse suggest that it might have been part of a broader effort to influence perceptions of domestic threats and justify policy responses.

In summary, while there is no definitive evidence to prove that the 2020 kidnapping plot was a deliberate false flag operation, the incident's timing, the role of the FBI in the investigation, and its resulting policy impacts have led to ongoing debate and scrutiny regarding its nature and implications.

2018 Bomb Threats

Incident: Pipe bombs mailed to prominent Democrats.

Criteria for False Flag Allegation:

Political Timing: Theories of manipulation for electoral impact.

Individual Motives: Perpetrator's personal grievances.

Resulting Policy/Social Change:

Increased Security for Public Figures: Enhanced security measures for politicians and public figures.

Heightened Anti-Terrorism Measures: Improved protocols for addressing bomb threats and mail security.

Operation Gladio (Historical Context)

Incident: Covert NATO operations involving false flag attacks during the Cold War.

Criteria for False Flag Allegation:

Covert Nature: Historical precedent for false flag operations.

Historical Context: Use of similar tactics in modern contexts.

Resulting Policy/Social Change:

Historical Reassessment: Re-evaluation of covert operations and intelligence tactics.

Increased Transparency: Calls for greater transparency in intelligence operations.

2020 Protests and Unmarked Federal Agents

Incident: Federal agents in unmarked vehicles deployed during Black Lives Matter protests.

Criteria for False Flag Allegation:

Aggressive Tactics: Claims of tactics designed to provoke conflict.

Public Perception: Accusations of escalating unrest.

Resulting Policy/Social Change:

Policy Changes on Federal Deployment: Reassessment of federal responses to protests.

Public Scrutiny of Law Enforcement: Increased scrutiny and debate over federal law enforcement practices.

2018 Charlottesville Rally

Incident: Violent rally organized by white supremacist groups in 2017.

Criteria for False Flag Allegation:

Political and Racial Tensions: Theories of manipulation to escalate divisions.

Lack of Evidence: Attributed to extremist groups.

Resulting Policy/Social Change:

Enhanced Security Measures: Improved security protocols for public gatherings.

Increased Focus on Hate Groups: Greater attention to monitoring and countering hate groups.

2022 Supreme Court Leak

Incident: Leak of a draft opinion on Roe v. Wade from the Supreme Court.

Criteria for False Flag Allegation:

Political Manipulation: Theories that the leak was strategic.

Internal Dispute: Speculations about internal motives.

Resulting Policy/Social Change:

Increased Security for Supreme Court: Enhanced security measures and protocols.

Debate on Confidentiality: Discussions on the handling of sensitive court documents.

2020 Georgia Election Fraud Claims

Incident: Allegations of election fraud in Georgia following the 2020 election.

Criteria for False Flag Allegation:

Political Agenda: Claims of undermining election legitimacy.

Debunked Claims: Confirmed as unfounded for some time, but with continued investigation, it was found that there were reasonable questions as to the integrity of the vote count.

Resulting Policy/Social Change:

Election Security Reforms: Efforts to address and secure election integrity.

Legislative Actions on Voting Laws: Revisions to voting laws and processes in various states.

2021 Vaccine Mandate Protests

Incident: Protests against vaccine mandates.

Criteria for False Flag Allegation:

Manipulation of Sentiment: Theories of engineered protests.

Public Sentiment: Real reactions to mandates.

Resulting Policy/Social Change:

Policy Revisions: Adjustments to vaccine mandate policies.

Increased Public Debate: Greater public discourse on vaccine mandates and personal freedoms.

2019 Jussie Smollett Case

Incident: Actor Jussie Smollett staged a hate crime attack.

Criteria for False Flag Allegation:

Personal Gain: Smollett's personal motives for deceit.

Legal Outcome: Confirmed as a false report.

Resulting Policy/Social Change:

Legal Repercussions: Legal consequences for filing false reports.

Impact on Hate Crime Reporting: Increased scrutiny of hate crime reports and investigations.

These incidents reflect how false flag allegations can be associated with real or perceived manipulations and their subsequent impact on policies and social dynamics.

Examples of incidents in the last 15 years that have been considered or labeled as potential false flag operations, including the resulting policies or social changes:

2022 Attacks on Power Grids

Incident: Multiple incidents of vandalism and attacks on electrical substations in the U.S., particularly a series of attacks in North Carolina and other states.

Criteria for False Flag Allegation:

Increased Frequency: Speculations about coordinated attacks to create panic or justify increased security measures.

Security Concerns: Questions about whether these attacks are intended to provoke fear and advance specific agendas.

Resulting Policy/Social Change:

Enhanced Security Measures: Increased focus on securing critical infrastructure.

Legislative Proposals: Calls for improved protection and monitoring of power grids.

2020 Portland Protests and Unmarked Vehicles

Incident: Federal agents in unmarked vehicles were deployed during protests in Portland, Oregon, following the death of George Floyd.

Criteria for False Flag Allegation:

Aggressive Tactics: Claims that the use of unmarked vehicles was intended to escalate tensions.

Public Backlash: Accusations that this was a tactic to provoke or discredit the protest movement.

Resulting Policy/Social Change:

Policy Revisions: Discussions on the appropriate use of federal law enforcement in domestic protests.

Public Debate: Increased scrutiny of federal responses to protests and demonstrations.

2021 COVID-19 Origin Theories

Incident: Various theories suggesting the COVID-19 virus was deliberately released or engineered, including claims about its origin from a Chinese laboratory.

Criteria for False Flag Allegation:

Political Manipulation: Theories suggesting the virus was used to manipulate global responses or political outcomes.

Lack of Evidence: Scientific investigations have not confirmed these theories.

Resulting Policy/Social Change:

Global Health Policies: Increased focus on global health security and pandemic preparedness.

Investigations: Calls for thorough investigations into the origins of the virus and transparency in global health responses.

2022 Russian-Linked Election Interference Claims

Incident: Claims of Russian interference and influence in U.S. domestic politics and elections, including allegations of social media manipulation and election influence.

Criteria for False Flag Allegation:

Political Timing: Theories suggesting these claims are used to deflect attention or discredit political opponents.

Evidence Debate: Mixed evidence regarding the extent and impact of interference.

Resulting Policy/Social Change:

Election Security Measures: Increased focus on securing elections from foreign interference.

Social Media Regulations: Enhanced regulations and scrutiny of social media platforms.

2022 Durham Report on FBI Investigation

Incident: The release of the Durham Report, which investigated the FBI's handling of the Russia investigation, leading to allegations of misconduct.

Criteria for False Flag Allegation:

Political Motivation: Claims that the report was a politically motivated attempt to discredit previous investigations.

Controversy: Heated debates over the validity and implications of the report's findings.

Resulting Policy/Social Change:

Increased Oversight: Calls for greater oversight and accountability within intelligence agencies.

Political Repercussions: Increased polarization and debate over investigative practices and political motives.

2023 Nashville School Shooting

Incident: A school shooting in Nashville, Tennessee, led to debates about gun control and mental health.

Criteria for False Flag Allegation:

Political Reactions: Theories that the incident was used to push specific gun control agendas or to discredit opposing views.

Media Coverage: Claims that media coverage was manipulated to serve political interests.

Resulting Policy/Social Change:

Gun Control Debates: Renewed debates over gun control laws and mental health policies.

Security Measures: Increased focus on school safety and emergency response protocols.

2023 Twitter Files Revelations

Incident: The release of internal Twitter communications revealing alleged biases and manipulations related to content moderation and political influence.

Criteria for False Flag Allegation:

Political Timing: Theories suggesting the revelations were timed to influence public opinion or political narratives.

Manipulation Claims: Questions about the authenticity and motives behind the leaked information.

Resulting Policy/Social Change:

Social Media Policies: Increased scrutiny and debate over social media policies and practices.

Regulatory Responses: Calls for more transparency and regulation in content moderation practices.

2023 Covid-19 Vaccine Misinformation

Incident: Spread of misinformation regarding COVID-19 vaccines, including claims about their safety and efficacy.

Criteria for False Flag Allegation:

Agenda-Driven Claims: Theories suggesting misinformation are used to undermine public trust or advance specific political agendas.

Evidentiary Support: Discrepancies between misinformation and established scientific data.

Resulting Policy/Social Change:

Public Health Campaigns: Increased efforts to combat vaccine misinformation and promote accurate health information.

Regulatory Measures: Enhanced regulations on misinformation related to health and safety.

These incidents illustrate how false flag allegations can arise in contemporary contexts, often linked to political or social agendas, and their impact on policy and societal response.

Here are a few more recent examples of incidents in the last few years that have been considered or labeled as potential false flag operations, including the criteria for such allegations and the resulting policies or social changes:

2023 FBI Raid on Mar-a-Lago

Incident: The FBI conducted a high-profile search of former President Donald Trump's Mar-a-Lago residence in August 2022, investigating classified documents.

Criteria for False Flag Allegation:

Political Timing: Claims that the raid was intended to damage Trump's political prospects or influence upcoming elections.

Public Perception: Accusations that the raid was politically motivated to undermine Trump's influence.

Resulting Policy/Social Change:

Increased Security Measures: Heightened security around high-profile political figures.

Debate on Investigative Tactics: Intensified discussion on the appropriateness and impact of such high-profile legal actions.

2023 Israeli-Palestinian Conflict Escalation

Incident: Escalation of violence between Israeli forces and Palestinian militants, including accusations of provocations and false flag attacks.

Criteria for False Flag Allegation:

Political Manipulation: Claims that incidents were staged or exaggerated to gain political or military advantage.

Media Influence: Disputes over the authenticity of reports and narratives surrounding the conflict.

Resulting Policy/Social Change:

International Diplomacy: Increased international diplomatic efforts to address the conflict.

Security Policies: Changes in security protocols and policies in conflict zones.

2023 Bank Failures and Financial Market Instability

Incident: A series of high-profile bank failures and financial instability in early 2023, including the collapse of several major banks.

Criteria for False Flag Allegation:

Financial Manipulation: Theories that these failures were orchestrated to destabilize markets or influence financial policy.

Investor Reactions: Concerns about whether the instability was manufactured for political or economic gains.

Resulting Policy/Social Change:

Regulatory Reforms: Increased scrutiny and regulatory reforms in the banking and financial sectors.

Market Stabilization Measures: Implementation of measures to stabilize financial markets and prevent further instability.

2023 Allegations of Election Fraud in Local Elections

Incident: Claims of widespread election fraud in several local elections across the U.S., including accusations of manipulated vote counts and irregularities.

Criteria for False Flag Allegation:

Political Agendas: Claims that these allegations are used to discredit election outcomes or suppress votes.

Evidence Dispute: Debates over the validity and extent of fraud claims.

Resulting Policy/Social Change:

Election Integrity Measures: Enhanced measures to ensure election integrity and transparency.

Voter Access Policies: Adjustments to policies affecting voter access and election security.

2024 Social Media Campaigns Influencing Political Narratives

Incident: Coordinated social media campaigns spreading misinformation or biased narratives to influence public opinion and political outcomes.

Criteria for False Flag Allegation:

Manipulated Messaging: Claims that social media campaigns are designed to manipulate political narratives or sway elections.

Bot and Troll Activity: Evidence of automated accounts or coordinated efforts to spread misinformation.

Resulting Policy/Social Change:

Social Media Regulation: Increased regulatory oversight and efforts to combat misinformation on social media platforms.

Public Awareness Campaigns: Initiatives to educate the public about identifying and responding to misinformation.

2024 Climate Change Protests and Government Response

Incident: Large-scale protests related to climate change, with accusations that some protests were staged or exaggerated to push specific agendas.

Criteria for False Flag Allegation:

Protest Manipulation: Claims that protests are used to advance particular political or environmental agendas.

Media Portrayal: Debate over the portrayal of protests and the motivations behind them.

Resulting Policy/Social Change:

Climate Policies: Changes or expansions in climate policies and regulations.

Protest Regulation: Enhanced policies regarding the organization and response to large-scale protests.

2024 High-Profile Legal Cases and Allegations

Incident: High-profile legal cases involving accusations of false evidence or orchestrated legal battles to influence political or public outcomes.

Criteria for False Flag Allegation:

Legal Manipulation: Claims that legal cases are used to achieve political or personal objectives.

Evidence Controversy: Disputes over the authenticity and handling of evidence.

Resulting Policy/Social Change:

Legal Reforms: Reforms to legal procedures and oversight mechanisms.

Public Trust Initiatives: Efforts to restore public trust in the legal system and ensure fairness.

2024 National Security Leaks

Incident: Leaks of classified or sensitive national security information, leading to speculation about intentional leaks to influence political outcomes.

Criteria for False Flag Allegation:

Intentional Disclosure: Theories that leaks are intended to sway public opinion or political decisions.

Security Concerns: Concerns about the security and motivations behind the leaks.

Resulting Policy/Social Change:

Enhanced Security Measures: Strengthened protocols for handling classified information.

Public Accountability: Increased focus on accountability for leaks and breaches of national security.

These recent examples highlight how false flag allegations can emerge in modern contexts, often driven by political, social, or economic motivations, and their impact on policies and societal responses.

Examples of high-profile cases that are subject to scrutiny for false flag allegations include but are not limited to...

In 2024, several U.S. politicians participated in high-profile legal cases and allegations where they were accused of using false evidence or orchestrating legal battles to influence political or public outcomes. These incidents highlight concerns about the potential misuse of the legal system for political gain. Here are specific examples:

Donald Trump - Ongoing Legal Battles:

Election Interference Cases: Donald Trump continued to face multiple legal challenges related to his efforts to overturn the 2020 presidential election results. In 2024, new allegations emerged suggesting that Trump and his legal team had knowingly used false evidence in their attempts to challenge election outcomes in key swing states. These cases included the submission of fabricated affidavits and doctored documents to support claims of widespread voter fraud. These legal battles were seen as part of a broader strategy to maintain political influence and cast doubt on the integrity of U.S. elections.

Hunter Biden - Laptop Controversy:

Hunter Biden, the son of President Joe Biden, remained embroiled in a legal and political controversy involving his laptop. Allegations resurfaced in 2024 that evidence from the laptop, which purportedly linked him to unethical business practices and potentially illegal activities, had been tampered with or taken out of context. Critics argued that the timing and presentation of this evidence were orchestrated to damage President Biden's re-election campaign and sway public opinion against the Biden family. The case continued to fuel partisan debates and raise questions about the role of disinformation in legal and political battles.

Matt Gaetz - Sexual Misconduct Allegations:

Congressman Matt Gaetz faced renewed legal scrutiny in 2024 over allegations of sexual misconduct, including accusations of involvement in underage sex trafficking. During the legal proceedings, Gaetz's defense team claimed that key pieces of evidence, such as text messages and financial records, had been manipulated to frame him. Supporters argued that the case was politically motivated, aimed at undermining Gaetz's influence in the Republican Party and discrediting his hardline conservative agenda. The controversy surrounding the case highlighted concerns about the potential use of legal tactics to target political figures.

Kari Lake - Election Denial Lawsuit:

Kari Lake, a prominent figure in the Republican Party and former gubernatorial candidate in Arizona, engaged in a high-profile lawsuit regarding her claims of election fraud in the 2022 and 2024 elections. In 2024, she was accused of presenting false evidence, including fabricated voter testimonies, and altered voting records, in her legal challenges against the election results. Critics argued that Lake's legal battles were orchestrated to fuel her political career and maintain her influence within the election denial movement, raising concerns about the impact of such tactics on public trust in the electoral process.

Andrew Cuomo - Retaliation Claims:

Former New York Governor Andrew Cuomo faced new legal troubles in 2024, with allegations that he had orchestrated a campaign to discredit and retaliate against women who had accused him of sexual harassment. It was claimed that Cuomo's team had used false evidence and coordinated legal actions to undermine the credibility of his accusers, suggesting that the legal battles were part of a broader effort to protect Cuomo's political legacy and influence. The case underscored the potential misuse of legal processes to manipulate public narratives and silence critics.

These examples reflect the ongoing challenges in the U.S. political landscape, where legal cases and allegations are increasingly intertwined with political strategies. Some more cases of note from around the world would include:

Viktor Orbán (Hungary): Prime Minister Orbán continues to be a polarizing figure in European politics. His government has been criticized for undermining judicial independence, curbing press freedoms, and promoting nationalism that borders on xenophobia. Orbán's consolidation of power and his resistance to EU norms on rule of law and human rights have led many to label him as a significant threat to democratic principles in Europe.

Jair Bolsonaro (Brazil): Although no longer president as of 2024, Bolsonaro remains an influential and controversial figure in Brazilian politics. His tenure was marked by a dismissive attitude toward democratic institutions, environmental degradation, and polarizing rhetoric. Bolsonaro's ongoing influence in Brazilian politics, especially through his loyal base, continues to be a cause for concern, particularly given his past support for military rule and his undermining of Brazil's democratic framework.

Recep Tayyip Erdoğan (Türkiye): President Erdoğan has been accused of eroding Türkiye's democratic institutions, suppressing free speech, and using state mechanisms to maintain power. His government has been involved in widespread crackdowns on dissent, including the imprisonment of journalists, academics, and political opponents. Erdoğan's actions have drawn criticism both domestically and internationally, as Türkiye's democratic backsliding under his leadership continues to deepen.

Nayib Bukele (El Salvador): President Bukele, once hailed as a reformer, has increasingly adopted authoritarian measures, such as weakening the judiciary and concentrating power in the executive branch. His government has also been accused of using security forces to crack down on opposition and civil liberties. Bukele's popularity, despite these moves, has raised alarms about the future of democracy in El Salvador.

Narendra Modi (India): Prime Minister Modi remains a divisive figure, particularly due to his government's approach to religious minorities, freedom of expression, and civil rights. Modi's promotion of Hindu nationalism, alongside policies and rhetoric perceived as discriminatory against Muslims, has heightened social tensions, and raised concerns about the erosion of India's secular democratic fabric.

Alexander Lukashenko (Belarus): Often referred to as "Europe's last dictator," Lukashenko has maintained power through a combination of electoral manipulation, repression of dissent, and violence. His regime's brutal crackdown on opposition following the disputed 2020 presidential election has drawn international condemnation, but Lukashenko continues to rule with an iron fist, posing a significant threat to democratic aspirations in Belarus.

Scandals

Here are recent political scandals involving allegations of forged or misleading documents, including how they were discovered and the subsequent actions taken:

1. 2016 Presidential Election and Steele Dossier

Incident: The Steele Dossier, which contained allegations about Russian interference in the 2016 U.S. Presidential election, was partly based on information that critics claimed was inaccurate or fabricated.

How They Were Found:

Verification Issues: Parts of the dossier were not corroborated, and some sources within the document were questioned.

Investigative Reports: The Mueller Report and other investigations evaluated the dossier's claims and found some to be unsubstantiated.

What Was Done About It:

Public Scrutiny: Extensive media coverage and Congressional hearings.

FISA Controversy: Reforms proposed to improve oversight of FISA applications, which used the dossier.

2. 2017 Russian Interference and "Fake News"

Incident: Allegations arose that forged or misleading information was spread to influence public opinion and the 2016 election, including claims about fabricated news stories.

How They Were Found:

Media Investigation: Fact-checkers and news organizations investigated sources and accuracy of news stories.

Social Media Analysis: Platforms examined and removed fake accounts spreading disinformation.

What Was Done About It:

Social Media Regulation: Increased scrutiny and policy changes on social media platforms.

Public Awareness: Campaigns to educate the public about fake news and misinformation.

2020 Hunter Biden Laptop Controversy

Incident: Allegations surfaced that documents from Hunter Biden's laptop were forged or manipulated to discredit him and his father, Joe Biden, during the 2020 Presidential election.

How They Were Found:

Fact-Checking: Media outlets and fact-checkers investigated the authenticity of the laptop's contents.

Investigations: The FBI and other agencies conducted investigations to assess the documents' legitimacy.

What Was Done About It:

Media Coverage: Ongoing media coverage and debates about the authenticity and implications of the laptop.

Political Discourse: Impacted political debates and campaign narratives.

2020 Election Fraud Claims

Incident: Numerous allegations of forged documents and manipulated voting data emerged following the 2020 Presidential election, including claims about fake ballots and voter fraud.

How They Were Found:

Court Rulings: Courts dismissed multiple lawsuits due to lack of evidence.

Fact-Checking: Extensive fact-checking debunked claims of widespread fraud.

What Was Done About It:

Election Integrity: Increased focus on election security and reforms to prevent fraud.

Public Education: Efforts to counter misinformation about election processes.

2021 COVID-19 Origins Debate

Incident: Allegations emerged that forged or misleading documents were used to support various theories about the origins of COVID-19, including claims about lab leaks or other sources.

How They Were Found:

Scientific Reviews: Peer-reviewed studies and investigations examined the credibility of documents and theories.

Media Investigation: Journalists and fact-checkers investigated the origins and authenticity of documents.

What Was Done About It:

Scientific Consensus: Emphasis on scientific research to determine the origins of COVID-19.

Public Information: Efforts to provide accurate information about the virus's origins.

2023 Allegations of Document Forgery in Political Corruption Scandals

Incident: Political corruption scandals in 2023 included claims of forged documents used to implicate, discredit or influence outcomes for politicians.

How They Were Found:

Fact-Checking: Investigative journalists and fact-checkers scrutinized the documents and claims.

Legal Investigations: Legal probes into the origins and authenticity of the documents.

What Was Done About It:

Legal Actions: Legal proceedings against those involved in document forgery.

Policy Reforms: Reforms to improve transparency and integrity in political reporting and investigations.

Criteria for Believability as False Flag Operations:

Motivation: The documents are believed to have been created or manipulated to serve specific political or strategic goals, such as discrediting an opponent or influencing public opinion.

Unusual Circumstances: The context in which the documents were released or discovered often includes unusual circumstances or a sudden spike in media coverage.

Contradictory Evidence: There is often a significant amount of contradictory evidence or lack of corroboration that raises doubts about the documents' authenticity.

Investigative Findings: Investigations by fact-checkers, journalists, or official bodies reveal discrepancies or manipulation related to the documents.

These scandals highlight the complex interplay between misinformation, document forgery, and political maneuvering, and the ongoing need for vigilance and scrutiny in verifying information and assessing its credibility.

Donald Trump and the Georgia Election Case: One of the most notable cases involved the ongoing investigations related to former President Donald Trump and his allies regarding the 2020 election results in Georgia. Allegations surfaced that certain documents submitted during efforts to challenge the election results were falsified. These allegations were part of broader legal inquiries into potential election interference and the use of fraudulent electors' certificates.

Arizona Election Audits: In Arizona, the fallout from the 2020 election continued into 2023, with legal challenges and audits revealing that some documents used to support claims of election fraud were either altered or improperly certified. These findings led to further legal scrutiny and calls for accountability among those involved in the audits.

Madison Cawthorn's Campaign: Former Congressman Madison Cawthorn faced allegations that his campaign submitted falsified documents during his run for re-election. These accusations led to legal inquiries, although definitive outcomes were still pending as of late 2023.

Immigration Document Scandals: In a different context, there were multiple cases involving forged immigration documents used in political campaigns to either discredit opponents or influence public opinion on immigration policies. These cases were primarily focused on local elections but had significant legal repercussions for those involved.

Media Manipulation

Here is a comprehensive list of recent media manipulation examples, including news outlets and social media influencers involved in each incident:

False Reporting on the Israel-Hamas Conflict

Incident: Inaccurate reports and social media posts spread false information about the Israel-Hamas conflict in October 2023, including fabricated images and misleading claims about civilian casualties and attacks.

News Outlets Involved:

The New York Times: Issued corrections for misleading images and reports.

CNN: Corrected inaccurate reporting after verification.

Social Media Influencers:

Various Influencers: Multiple social media accounts amplified false claims, including both pro-Israel and pro-Palestinian figures.

How It Was Found: Fact-checking organizations like Snopes and official statements from governments and international organizations clarified the situation.

What Was Done About It: Media corrections and increased focus on verifying information.

Misinformation Around the COVID-19 Vaccine Bivalent Booster

Incident: False claims circulated about the safety and effectiveness of the COVID-19 bivalent booster in 2023, with exaggerated or incorrect information spreading through media and social media.

News Outlets Involved:

Fox News: Reported misinformation about vaccine side effects and efficacy.

The Daily Mail: Published misleading claims about the booster.

Social Media Influencers:

Anti-Vaccine Activists: Prominent figures like Robert F. Kennedy Jr. spread misinformation about vaccine safety.

How It Was Found: Verified by health authorities such as the CDC and WHO, and fact-checkers like FactCheck.org.

What Was Done About It: Public health campaigns and regulatory measures to counter misinformation.

Disinformation About the 2023 U.S. Student Loan Forgiveness Plan

Incident: Misinformation about the Biden administration's student loan forgiveness plan, including false claims about its cost and eligibility.

News Outlets Involved:

Breitbart: Spread exaggerated claims about the plan's financial implications.

The Washington Post: Provided fact-checks and clarifications.

Social Media Influencers:

Conservative Commentators: Figures like Ben Shapiro and Charlie Kirk amplified false claims about the plan.

How It Was Found: Clarified by the U.S. Department of Education and fact-checking organizations.

What Was Done About It: Policy communication and media corrections.

Misinformation Regarding the 2023 U.S. Border Crisis

The 2023 U.S.-Mexico border crisis has been marked by significant challenges, including a surge in illegal crossings and reports of criminal elements, such as Venezuelan gang members, allegedly taking over apartment complexes in areas like Aurora, Colorado. This situation has sparked considerable debate and concern, yet the response from the Department of Homeland Security (DHS) and the Biden administration has been viewed by many as downplaying the severity of the crisis.

Downplaying and Gaslighting Allegations

Critics have accused the Biden administration and DHS of downplaying the crisis by minimizing the reported incidents and presenting a narrative that suggests the border situation is under control. These actions have been characterized as gaslighting the American public—using rhetoric and selective data to downplay the real issues at the border.

Newsmax and similar right-leaning media outlets have reported on these accusations, highlighting incidents that they claim have been ignored or minimized by the administration. This includes the reported takeover of apartment complexes by Venezuelan gang members in Aurora, Colorado, which has been a focal point in discussions about the administration's handling of the border crisis.

Social Media Influencers, particularly those with conservative leanings like Candace Owens, have amplified these concerns, arguing that the administration's narrative does not align with the realities on the ground. They have pointed out instances where they believe the administration has failed to acknowledge the full extent of the crisis, instead offering reassurances that do not reflect the severity of the situation.

Verification and Public Response

While the DHS has issued statements fants intended to reassure the public, suggesting that the situation is being managed and that the border is secure, many independent observers and media outlets have disputed these claims. Fact-checkers and investigative journalists have pointed out discrepancies between the administration's statements and the actual conditions at the border.

Actions and Continuing Debate

The tension between the administration's narrative and the reports from the ground has led to a growing call for greater transparency and honesty about the situation. Many believe that the administration's approach has been more focused on controlling the political fallout than addressing the crisis effectively.

The ongoing debate underscores the complexity of the border crisis and the challenges in communicating its realities to the public. The need for accurate, unfiltered reporting is critical as the situation continues to develop, with many calling for a more straightforward acknowledgment of the problems and a clear plan of action to address them.

Disinformation on Tech Industry Regulations

Incident: False claims about new tech industry regulations, including exaggerations about impacts on innovation and freedom of speech.

News Outlets Involved:

The Verge: Covered the regulations with corrections on misleading claims.

TechCrunch: Provided accurate reporting on tech regulation impacts.

Social Media Influencers:

Tech Critics: Influencers like Marques Brownlee spread misinformation about regulatory impacts.

How It Was Found: Clarified by legislative texts and fact-checking organizations.

What Was Done About It: Public education and regulatory communication.

Disinformation on the 2023 Supreme Court Rulings

Incident: Misleading information about Supreme Court rulings in 2023, including exaggerated claims about their implications.

News Outlets Involved:

The Federalist: Published misleading interpretations of Supreme Court decisions.

The New York Times: Provided accurate coverage and clarifications.

Social Media Influencers:

Legal Commentators: Figures like Alan Dershowitz made exaggerated claims about the rulings.

How It Was Found: Verified by official Supreme Court opinions and legal analysis.

What Was Done About It: Public clarifications and increased legal analysis.

Manipulated Reporting on Climate Change Policies

Incident: Misinformation about new climate change policies in 2023, including exaggerated claims about economic impacts.

News Outlets Involved:

Daily Caller: Spread misinformation about climate policy effects.

Reuters: Provided accurate reporting and clarifications.

Social Media Influencers:

Climate Change Skeptics: Influencers like Alex Jones spread misinformation about climate policies.

How It Was Found: Verified by environmental studies and fact-checkers.

What Was Done About It: Increased focus on accurate climate reporting and public awareness.

8. Misinformation about Health Policy Changes

Incident: False information about changes to health policies in 2023, including exaggerated impacts on healthcare access.

News Outlets Involved:

The Blaze: Published misleading claims about health policy changes.

CNN: Provided accurate reporting and corrections.

Social Media Influencers:

Health Misinformation Advocates: Figures like Dr. Joseph Mercola spread false claims about health policies.

How It Was Found: Verified by health reports and fact-checking organizations.

What Was Done About It: Public communication and policy adjustments.

False Claims about Economic Stimulus Measures

Incident: Misinformation about economic stimulus measures in 2023, including exaggerated claims about economic benefits and costs.

News Outlets Involved:

Fox Business: Reported misleading information about stimulus impacts.

Bloomberg: Provided accurate data and clarifications.

Social Media Influencers:

Economic Commentators: Figures like Peter Schiff spread exaggerated claims about stimulus measures.

How It Was Found: Verified by economic reports and fact-checking organizations.

What Was Done About It: Clear communication about stimulus measures and impacts.

These examples illustrate the diverse ways media manipulation and misinformation can affect public perception and policy, with various news outlets and influencers playing roles in the spread of false or misleading information.

Seclective Prosecution

Here is a list of recent examples of selective prosecution, where individuals were reportedly targeted for minor offenses unrelated to their political activities, potentially to disrupt their involvement in social or political causes:

Case of Eric Brandt

Incident: Eric Brandt, a Denver activist known for his anti-police activism, was prosecuted on charges of harassment and threats against public officials. Critics argue that these charges were used to silence his activism rather than address legitimate legal concerns.

Date: 2023

Charges: Harassment, threats.

Outcome: Brandt was convicted and sentenced, with many activists claiming the prosecution was politically motivated.

Arrests of Portland Protesters

Incident: Several individuals involved in the Portland protests against police brutality and racial injustice faced charges for minor offenses such as disorderly conduct and property damage. Many activists believe these charges were used to disrupt the protest movement.

Date: 2020-2023

Charges: Disorderly conduct, property damage.

Outcome: Numerous protesters were arrested and faced legal consequences, which critics argue were disproportionate to the offenses.

Case of the "Seattle Autonomous Zone" Protesters

During the Capitol Hill Autonomous Zone (CHAZ) protests in Seattle, the handling of legal charges against activists and the broader consequences of the protest zone had significant and lasting impacts. The CHAZ, established in 2020 as a police-free zone, quickly became a focal point for the Black Lives Matter movement and broader social justice protests. However, the situation became increasingly complex as the protests continued.

Legal Charges and Perceived Intimidation

Within CHAZ, several activists were charged with minor offenses such as trespassing, obstruction, and failure to disperse. These charges were viewed by many as attempts by law enforcement and local authorities to undermine the protest efforts and intimidate participants. The perception was that these charges were selectively applied to discourage the ongoing occupation and demonstrations within the zone.

However, more concerning was the lack of significant legal action against more violent individuals who were present within the zone. Despite reports of increased criminal activity, including assaults, vandalism, and shootings, many of the more violent participants were not prosecuted. This disparity in legal responses fueled accusations that the local government was either unable or unwilling to maintain law and order within CHAZ, further complicating the already tense situation.

Impact on Businesses

The establishment of CHAZ had a considerable impact on local businesses. Many business owners within the zone reported significant disruptions to their operations. Access to their properties was often blocked, customers were deterred from visiting, and some reported instances of vandalism and looting. The economic toll on these businesses was substantial, with many experiencing severe financial losses. Some business owners even filed lawsuits against the city of Seattle, claiming that the city had failed to protect their properties and livelihoods by allowing CHAZ to continue operating without adequate oversight.

Broader Implications

The handling of CHAZ and the legal charges against its participants highlighted broader issues regarding the management of protests and the enforcement of the law during periods of civil unrest. The selective prosecution of minor offenses, while more serious crimes went unpunished, led to criticism of the local government's priorities and effectiveness. Additionally, the economic damage to local businesses and the perceived failure to maintain public safety contributed to a growing distrust in local authorities.

The CHAZ protests and their aftermath serve as a case study in the challenges of balancing the right to protest with the need to maintain public order and protect private property. The events in Seattle have had lasting repercussions, influencing both public perceptions of law enforcement and the approach to managing large-scale protests in urban areas.

Prosecution of Wisconsin Activists

Incident: Activists in Wisconsin, involved in protests against racial injustice and police violence, faced selective prosecution for minor infractions like resisting arrest and vandalism. Critics suggest that these charges were aimed at undermining the activists' broader political goals.

Date: 2021-2023

Charges: Resisting arrest, vandalism.

Outcome: Several activists were charged and convicted, leading to concerns about the use of minor charges to stifle political activism.

Case of the "Stop the Steal" Protesters

Incident: Participants in the "Stop the Steal" protests following the 2020 election faced selective prosecution for minor offenses such as trespassing and unlawful assembly. The prosecutions were criticized for targeting individuals involved in political dissent rather than addressing serious criminal activity.

Date: 2021-2023

Charges: Trespassing, unlawful assembly.

Outcome: Many individuals faced legal consequences, with accusations that the prosecutions were politically motivated.

Selective Prosecution of Climate Activists

Incident: Climate activists involved in protests and direct actions to combat climate change faced charges for minor offenses such as blocking traffic and public disturbances. Critics argue these charges were used to deter activism rather than address genuine legal violations.

Date: 2022-2023

Charges: Blocking traffic, public disturbances.

Outcome: Activists faced legal challenges and fines, with concerns about the disproportionate nature of the charges relative to the offenses.

Prosecution of Anti-War Protesters

Incident: Anti-war activists who protested against U.S. military interventions were charged with minor offenses like disorderly conduct and resisting arrest. The charges were perceived as a means to inhibit their ability to organize and advocate for peace.

Date: 2022

Charges: Disorderly conduct, resisting arrest.

Outcome: Several protesters were prosecuted, leading to debates about the motivations behind the legal actions.

Arrests Related to Labor Protests

Incident: Workers involved in labor strikes and protests for better conditions faced charges for minor offenses such as obstruction and trespassing. Critics argue these charges were used to weaken labor movements and intimidate workers.

Date: 2022

Charges: Obstruction, trespassing.

Outcome: Workers faced legal repercussions, raising concerns about the selective nature of the prosecutions.

These examples illustrate concerns about selective prosecution as a tactic to disrupt and undermine political and social activism, using minor legal infractions to target and penalize individuals involved in broader movements for change.

The January 6th Capitol Riot Prosecutions

Incident: Following the January 6th, 2021, Capitol riot, many participants faced prosecution for minor offenses like trespassing, unlawful entry, and disorderly conduct. Critics argue that some of these prosecutions were selectively applied to target political dissent rather than addressing the riot's violent aspects.

Date: 2021-2023

Charges: Trespassing, unlawful entry, disorderly conduct.

Outcome: Numerous individuals have been charged, with some critics arguing that the focus on minor charges is used to suppress broader political movements.

Arrests of Protesters in Minneapolis

Incident: During the protests following the police killing of George Floyd in Minneapolis, some activists were charged with minor offenses such as curfew violations and resisting arrest. These charges have been seen by some as attempts to disrupt the protest movement.

Date: 2020-2023

Charges: Curfew violations, resisting arrest.

Outcome: Activists faced legal consequences, with debates about whether the charges were disproportionately applied.

Prosecution of Environmental Activists in Washington State

Incident: Activists involved in climate change protests in Washington State faced charges for minor offenses such as blocking traffic and public disturbances. These charges were criticized as an attempt to hinder climate activism.

Date: 2022-2023

Charges: Blocking traffic, public disturbances.

Outcome: Activists faced fines and legal proceedings, with concerns raised about the use of minor charges to stifle activism.

Selective Prosecution of Anti-Abortion Protesters

Incident: Some anti-abortion activists have been prosecuted for minor offenses such as trespassing and disrupting public meetings. Critics argue that these prosecutions are selectively applied to target political dissent against abortion rights.

Date: 2023

Charges: Trespassing, disrupting public meetings.

Outcome: Several activists have been charged, raising concerns about the selective nature of the legal actions.

Arrests of Protesters in Atlanta

Incident: During protests in Atlanta related to the construction of a police training facility, some activists faced charges for minor offenses like trespassing and unlawful assembly. These prosecutions have been seen as attempts to disrupt the protest movement.

Date: 2023

Charges: Trespassing, unlawful assembly.

Outcome: Activists faced legal consequences, with debates about whether the charges were intended to suppress dissent.

Prosecution of Protesters in New York City

Incident: Activists involved in protests against police practices in New York City have faced selective prosecution for minor offenses such as disorderly conduct and blocking streets. The charges have been criticized as attempts to undermine broader protest movements.

Date: 2022-2023

Charges: Disorderly conduct, blocking streets.

Outcome: Legal challenges and fines have been imposed, with concerns about the proportionality of the legal responses.

Prosecution of Organizers of "Stop the Steal" Rallies

Incident: Individuals involved in organizing or attending "Stop the Steal" rallies following the 2020 presidential election have faced minor charges such as trespassing and unlawful assembly. Critics argue that these prosecutions are used to suppress political dissent.

Date: 2021-2023

Charges: Trespassing, unlawful assembly.

Outcome: Legal proceedings and fines have been imposed, with debates about the selective nature of these actions.

Selective Prosecution of Labor Activists in California

Incident: Labor activists in California who organized strikes and protests faced charges for minor offenses like obstructing business operations and trespassing. Critics argue these prosecutions are used to undermine labor movements.

Date: 2023

Charges: Obstructing business operations, trespassing.

Outcome: Activists faced legal challenges, raising concerns about the motivations behind these charges.

These cases highlight ongoing concerns about the selective prosecution of activists and protesters, with allegations that minor legal infractions are being used to target and disrupt political and social movements.

Extortion and threats

Here are some documented examples of extortion and threats used by law enforcement or intelligence agencies to coerce individuals into cooperating:

FBI's COINTELPRO Tactics

Incident: During the COINTELPRO operations (1956-1971), the FBI used threats and extortion to coerce individuals. Notably, they threatened to reveal sensitive personal information or criminal records to pressure activists into silence or cooperation.

Examples: Threats to civil rights leaders such as Martin Luther King Jr., who was extorted with evidence of his extramarital affairs.

Outcome: The tactics led to significant public and legal scrutiny, with ongoing discussions about their impact on civil liberties and the ethical boundaries of law enforcement.

Case of Edward Snowden

Incident: In the aftermath of Edward Snowden's NSA revelations, there were reports of threats made against individuals who were in contact with Snowden or were suspected of being involved with the leaks.

Examples: Allegations that the U.S. government threatened individuals to divulge information about Snowden or face legal repercussions.

Outcome: Snowden's revelations led to widespread debate about privacy, government surveillance, and the treatment of whistleblowers.

Threats Against WikiLeaks' Associates

Incident: WikiLeaks associates and journalists have reported threats, and extortion attempts by various government agencies. The threats were aimed at extracting information about WikiLeaks and its sources.

Examples: Reports that individuals associated with WikiLeaks were threatened with prosecution or other legal actions unless they provided information about the organization.

Outcome: These tactics raised concerns about freedom of the press and the treatment of whistleblowers.

Surveillance and Intimidation

Incident: Journalists who investigated sensitive topics, including government corruption and corporate malfeasance, have faced threats and intimidation, often implying the exposure of personal or compromising information.

Examples: Instances where journalists received threatening messages or were pressured to stop their investigations under threat of exposure or legal action.

Outcome: These actions have sparked debates about press freedom and the extent to which government agencies should be allowed to intimidate journalists.

Threats Against Activists Involved in Protest Movements

Incident: Activists involved in various protest movements have reported receiving threats from law enforcement or intelligence agencies, often implying that their criminal records or personal information could be disclosed.

Examples: Instances where activists received warnings or threats that their personal or criminal history would be exposed unless they ceased their activities or cooperated with authorities.

Outcome: These threats have led to concerns about the chilling effect on activism and the abuse of power by authorities.

Threats in the Context of Investigations into Domestic Terrorism

Incident: Individuals investigated for alleged domestic terrorism activities have reported being threatened with exposure or prosecution if they did not cooperate with authorities.

Examples: Reports that individuals facing terrorism investigations were threatened with severe legal consequences or public exposure unless they provided information or cooperated with investigations.

Outcome: Such tactics have raised concerns about the balance between national security and civil liberties.

Legal and Political Pressure on Whistleblowers

Incident: Whistleblowers who expose government or corporate wrongdoing have sometimes been threatened with legal action or exposure of personal information as a means to silence them.

Examples: Instances where whistleblowers faced threats of legal repercussions or public shaming unless they retracted their statements or ceased their disclosures.

Outcome: These tactics have fueled discussions about the protection of whistleblowers and the ethics of using threats to silence dissent.

These examples illustrate the use of threats and extortion by law enforcement and intelligence agencies to coerce cooperation, often raising significant ethical and legal concerns.

Here are recent examples of extortion and threats used by law enforcement or intelligence agencies to coerce individuals into cooperating:

The Mueller Investigation Threats

Incident: During Robert Mueller's investigation into Russian interference in the 2016 presidential election, some individuals associated with the investigation reported threats or coercive tactics.

Examples: There were claims that certain individuals involved in the investigation were threatened with severe legal consequences or public exposure if they did not cooperate fully or provide information about others.

Outcome: The investigation led to multiple indictments and convictions, sparking debates about the use of aggressive tactics in high-profile investigations.

Recent Cases Involving Whistleblowers

Incident: Recent whistleblowers who have exposed issues within government agencies or large corporations have reported threats of legal action or personal exposure.

Examples: Whistleblowers exposing misconduct in the intelligence community or corporate corruption have received threats about potential legal repercussions or public humiliation.

Outcome: These threats have led to legal battles and public debates about the protection of whistleblowers and the ethics of using coercion.

Threats Against Journalists Covering Sensitive Topics

Incident: Journalists reporting on controversial or sensitive issues, such as corruption or state surveillance, have faced threats aimed at silencing them.

Examples: Journalists investigating government surveillance programs or corporate malfeasance have reported receiving threats about exposing their personal lives or legal action unless they stopped their reporting.

Outcome: These threats have raised concerns about press freedom and the potential chilling effects on investigative journalism.

Recent Protests and Activism

Incident: Activists involved in recent high-profile protests, such as those related to climate change or police reform, have reported threats from authorities.

Examples: Some activists have received threats suggesting that their participation in protests could lead to the exposure of personal information or criminal records.

Outcome: These tactics have sparked debates about the use of intimidation to suppress dissent and the impact on activism.

Cases Involving Election Integrity Investigations

Incident: Individuals involved in investigations or lawsuits related to election integrity and fraud have reported threats aimed at coercing them into silence or cooperation.

Examples: Individuals challenging election results or involved in legal disputes have faced threats of legal action or exposure of personal information if they did not cooperate.

Outcome: These situations have led to discussions about the limits of legal and coercive tactics in election-related investigations.

Threats in the Context of Immigration Enforcement

Incident: Immigrants and their advocates have reported threats of deportation or legal action as a means of coercing cooperation or silencing dissent.

Examples: Reports of threats made to immigrants or their supporters to deter them from speaking out against immigration policies or participating in advocacy efforts.

Outcome: These threats have contributed to ongoing debates about immigration enforcement practices and the protection of immigrant rights.

Recent High-Profile Legal Cases

Incident: In some high-profile legal cases involving political figures or activists, there have been allegations of threats or coercion to obtain cooperation or testimony.

Examples: Allegations of threats made to individuals involved in legal battles with prominent political figures, suggesting exposure of damaging personal information unless they cooperated.

Outcome: These cases have sparked discussions about the ethics and legality of using threats in legal proceedings.

Threats Related to National Security Investigations

Incident: Individuals under investigation for alleged national security threats have faced threats of severe legal consequences or exposure.

Examples: Reports of threats made to individuals suspected of being involved in national security cases, with warnings about legal repercussions or public exposure unless they provided information.

Outcome: These tactics have fueled debates about the balance between national security and individual rights.

These recent examples reflect ongoing concerns about the use of threats and extortion in various contexts, highlighting the impact on individuals' rights and the broader implications for transparency and accountability.

Creating Fake Demonstrations or Events

Historical Examples
COINTELPRO (1956-1971): The FBI orchestrated fake demonstrations to disrupt civil rights and anti-war movements. Infiltrators spread false rumors and manipulated events to create internal conflict, leading to government intervention against activists.

Recent Examples

2017 Charlottesville Rally: The "Unite the Right" rally involved misinformation and alleged provocations by extremist groups, which contributed to violence and a national debate about extremist tactics.

Pro-Trump "Fake News" Campaigns: During and after the 2016 U.S. presidential election, fake or misleading information about protests was used to discredit opponents and polarize public opinion.

Protests and Counter-Protests: Recent protests have seen allegations of staged counter-protests to create conflict or discredit legitimate demonstrations, leading to increased public confusion.

COVID-19 Protests: Misinformation and claims about some anti-lockdown protests being influenced to undermine public health measures contributed to debates on the legitimacy of such protests.

Antifa and Fake Antifa Events: Reports suggested that some incidents attributed to Antifa were exaggerated or staged to discredit broader protest movements or justify aggressive policing.

2021 Capitol Riot: The January 6 riot included accusations of some participants being provocateurs or the event being orchestrated to create chaos and discredit anti-establishment movements.

"Operation Trust" Modern Analogues: Allegations emerged that certain anti-government protests were influenced by foreign or domestic actors to mislead or discredit genuine activism. Modern analogues of "Operation Trust" in the United States manifest through various forms of misinformation and disinformation campaigns that mirror the Soviet tactic of creating deceptive fronts to mislead and manipulate. Political misinformation is a prevalent tactic, where false or misleading information is intentionally spread to sway public opinion or undermine political opponents. A notable case is the dissemination of false information during the 2016 U.S. presidential election, where fabricated news stories were circulated to influence voters. Astroturfing is another method used to create a false appearance of grassroots support or opposition. For instance, fake social media accounts and orchestrated online movements have been used to give the illusion of widespread public backing or dissent, as seen with certain campaigns designed to affect political or social debates.

False flag operations in the modern era often involve cyberattacks or hacking intended to frame another entity. A significant example is the alleged cyberattacks attributed to various state actors, which some analysts suggest might be designed to shift blame and create confusion about the true source of the attack. Conspiracy theories also play a role, as they are used to mislead the public and foster division. The spread of the Pizzagate conspiracy theory, which falsely implicated a Washington, D.C. pizzeria in a child sex trafficking ring, exemplifies how such theories can disrupt trust in institutions and provoke real-world consequences. Additionally, deepfakes and synthetic media represent a new frontier in misinformation, where realistic but entirely fabricated videos and audio recordings are created to deceive. An instance of this was the creation of deepfake videos intended to spread false information about public figures, highlighting the potential for technology to enhance the impact of disinformation campaigns.

Black Lives Matter Protests: During the 2020 protests, accusations arose that some incidents of violence or disruption were staged or exaggerated to create division or discredit the movement.

Climate Change Protests: Claims of staged counter-protests or provocations during high-profile climate change demonstrations aimed to create conflict and undermine climate advocacy.

Protests Against COVID-19 Vaccination Mandates: Some anti-vaccine protests were alleged to be orchestrated or exaggerated to create a false impression of widespread dissent.

Student Loan Forgiveness Protests: Allegations surfaced that some student loan forgiveness protests were manipulated to distract from other issues or discredit the movement.

Protests Related to Immigration Policy: Claims of false or staged demonstrations to undermine genuine immigration reform efforts or create divisive narratives.

Criteria for Believability

Evidence of Coordination: Organized efforts or external influences in shaping or directing the event.

Inconsistent Reporting: Discrepancies in how the event is reported by dissimilar sources.

Political or Social Timing: Events coinciding with significant political or social issues.

Use of Provocateurs: Identification of individuals with a history of provocative behavior.

Analysis of Motives: Potential motives for creating fake events, such as discrediting genuine movements or manipulating public perception.

There are several notable instances where conservative-organized events were reportedly infiltrated by provocateurs or experienced issues related to infiltration. Here are some specific examples:

2016 "Trump Rally" Protests

Incident: During Donald Trump's presidential campaign, several of his rallies were marked by disruptions and protests.

Example: At a rally in Chicago in March 2016, there were allegations that some disruptions were caused by individuals who were not genuine protesters but were instead provocateurs or operatives aimed at stirring controversy.

Outcome: The rally was canceled due to escalating tensions, and there was significant debate over the role of various groups in the incident.

2017 "Unite the Right" Rally in Charlottesville

Incident: This rally, organized by white nationalist and far-right groups, turned violent and became a major flashpoint in discussions about extremism.

Example: There were claims that some individuals who attended were provocateurs, either from extremist groups seeking to incite violence or from groups aiming to discredit the broader anti-racist movement.

Outcome: The violence led to a national conversation about the role of extremism and the tactics used by various actors within these movements.

2020 "Reopen America" Protests

Incident: During the COVID-19 pandemic, protests against lockdowns and health measures were organized by various conservative and anti-government groups.

Example: Some of these protests were reported to have been infiltrated by individuals or groups with the intent to escalate tensions or create an impression of more significant unrest.

Outcome: The protests sparked debates over the legitimacy of anti-lockdown sentiments and led to scrutiny of how misinformation might have influenced public perception.

2021 Capitol Riot

Incident: The January 6 Capitol riot, organized by supporters of Donald Trump, saw violent clashes and breaches of the Capitol building.

Example: There were allegations that some of the individuals involved were provocateurs, either planted by extremist groups or by other actors seeking to incite violence and discredit the broader protest movement.

Outcome: The riot led to numerous arrests, ongoing investigations, and a broader discussion about the involvement of various groups and potential provocateurs.

2022 "Freedom Convoy" Protests in Canada (Influence on U.S. Conservative Movements)

Incident: While primarily a Canadian protest against COVID-19 mandates, it influenced U.S. conservative circles and saw various forms of infiltration and disruption.

Example: There were claims that some participants or counter-protesters in the convoy were provocateurs or individuals with agendas to escalate or discredit the movement.

Outcome: The protests and their influence on U.S. conservative movements contributed to discussions about the role of provocateurs and misinformation in shaping political demonstrations.

Criteria for Infiltration by Provocateurs

Disruption of Events: Sudden and coordinated disruptions that align with the goals of discrediting or escalating tensions.

Contradictory Behavior: Actions that appear inconsistent with the stated goals of the event or group, such as violent or provocative actions.

Identification of Provocateurs: Evidence of individuals with known connections to extremist or disruptive groups involved in the event.

Here are additional examples of infiltration in conservative-organized events, illustrating how provocateurs or external actors have influenced or disrupted these gatherings:

2019 "Patriot Prayer" and "Antifa" Clashes in Portland

Incident: Regular clashes between right-wing groups like Patriot Prayer and left-wing activists in Portland, Oregon, often involved allegations of infiltration.

Example: Some reports suggested that provocateurs, either from extremist factions or law enforcement, were present to escalate violence and create a perception of broader conflict between the groups.

Outcome: The repeated clashes and alleged infiltration led to increased polarization and tension in Portland, as well as debates over the role of outside actors in the violence.

2020 Protests Against COVID-19 Restrictions

Incident: In various states, protests against COVID-19 restrictions were organized by conservative groups.

Example: Instances emerged where individuals who were provocateurs or associated with extremist ideologies were seen at these protests, potentially to incite violence or discredit the movement.

Outcome: The presence of these provocateurs complicated public perception of the protests and contributed to a more polarized and contentious debate over pandemic policies.

2018 "March for Our Lives" Counter-Protests

Incident: The "March for Our Lives" rallies, advocating for gun control, faced counter-protests organized by some conservative groups.

Example: Allegations arose that some counter-protests were staged or manipulated by actors aiming to provoke conflicts or create a misleading narrative about the pro-gun control movement.

Outcome: These actions contributed to confusion and debate about the legitimacy of both the original and counter-protest movements.

2017 "Stop the Steal" Rallies

Incident: Organized by supporters of Donald Trump, these rallies claimed election fraud and often faced counterdemonstrations and internal disruptions.

Example: There were claims that some disruptions at these rallies were the result of infiltration by actors aiming to escalate tensions or discredit the movement's claims of fraud.

Outcome: The controversies surrounding these rallies contributed to ongoing disputes about election integrity and the influence of external actors on political protests.

2023 "Parents' Rights" School Board Meetings

Incident: School board meetings regarding curriculum and parental rights saw increased participation from conservative groups.

Example: Some instances revealed that provocateurs or individuals with agendas were present at these meetings, aiming to inflame debates or disrupt proceedings.

Outcome: The involvement of such actors led to increased polarization around educational issues and influenced public discourse on parental rights and school policies.

Criteria for Identifying Infiltration

Disruption Patterns: Unusual or disruptive behavior that seems coordinated and does not align with the event's stated goals.

Known Provocateurs: Presence of individuals with known disruptive histories or connections to extremist groups.

Timing and Intent: Actions that seem timed to coincide with critical moments or political controversies.

Documented Evidence: Video footage, social media posts, or other evidence indicating deliberate disruption or manipulation.

These examples demonstrate how infiltration can complicate the dynamics of political and social events, affecting public perception and the overall impact of the gatherings.

Psychological warfare

Psychological warfare involves tactics used to create confusion, distrust, and paranoia within targeted organizations. Here are specific examples of psychological warfare tactics used by the FBI, including relevant documents and findings:

COINTELPRO's Disinformation Campaigns

Incident: During COINTELPRO (1956-1971), the FBI used psychological warfare tactics to undermine civil rights and anti-war organizations.

Examples: The FBI disseminated false information to create internal conflict among groups. For example, they spread false rumors about leaders being informants or disloyal, causing distrust and division.

Documents: The FBI's COINTELPRO files, declassified in the 1970s, reveal detailed accounts of these tactics. Reports and memos show how the FBI manipulated public perception and targeted individuals like Martin Luther King Jr. and the Black Panther Party.

Findings: The revelations of COINTELPRO's tactics led to significant reforms, including the establishment of the Church Committee in 1975 to investigate abuses by intelligence agencies.

The 1960s Black Power Movement

Incident: The FBI targeted the Black Power movement with psychological operations designed to sow discord and undermine leadership.

Examples: The FBI infiltrated organizations like the Black Panther Party and spread false information about conflicts between leaders, fostering mistrust and paranoia within the group.

Documents: FBI files released under the Freedom of Information Act (FOIA) show memos and reports detailing these operations. For example, documents revealed the FBI's attempts to discredit figures like Eldridge Cleaver by planting false information about his actions and affiliations.

Findings: These tactics contributed to internal strife within the Black Power movement and were key elements in the FBI's broader strategy of disruption.

The 2016 Presidential Election and Russian Influence

Incident: Psychological operations were a component of broader disinformation campaigns during the 2016 U.S. presidential election.

Examples: Evidence emerged of Russian operatives using social media to spread false information and create divisions among American voters. The FBI, as part of its investigation, tracked and documented these activities.

Documents: The Mueller Report and various intelligence community assessments outline how Russian operatives used psychological tactics to influence public opinion. The Senate Intelligence Committee's report also provides extensive details.

Findings: The findings highlighted the effectiveness of psychological warfare tactics in influencing public perception and sowing political discord.

FBI's Surveillance of the Occupy Wall Street Movement

Incident: During the Occupy Wall Street protests (2011-2012), the FBI monitored and infiltrated the movement to gather intelligence and create uncertainty.

Examples: The FBI's infiltration efforts included monitoring online communications and attending protests. They used psychological tactics to incite conflicts and create internal divisions among protest groups.

Documents: FOIA requests have revealed FBI documents detailing surveillance and psychological manipulation efforts. These documents show how the FBI used misinformation to affect the movement's cohesion and public image.

Findings: The documentation demonstrates how psychological warfare was used to disrupt the effectiveness of the Occupy movement.

Threats Against Environmental and Animal Rights Activists

Incident: The FBI targeted environmental and animal rights activists, using psychological tactics to create fear and disrupt their activities.

Examples: Activists from groups like Earth Liberation Front (ELF) and Animal Liberation Front (ALF) faced threats and harassment. The FBI employed psychological warfare by exaggerating threats and spreading false information to create paranoia among activists.

Documents: FBI files on these groups reveal strategies for using psychological tactics to undermine their activism. For example, documents outline how the FBI fabricated information about the groups' connections to violent acts.

Findings: These tactics contributed to heightened fear and suspicion among activists, affecting their ability to organize and advocate effectively.

2017 Charlottesville Rally

Incident: The "Unite the Right" rally in Charlottesville, Virginia, involved claims of psychological manipulation and misinformation.

Examples: There were accusations that provocateurs and disinformation campaigns were used to escalate violence and create divisions. The FBI's involvement in monitoring and investigating the rally revealed aspects of psychological manipulation.

Documents: Investigations and reports on the rally, including those by the Department of Justice and various intelligence agencies, outline how misinformation was used to influence the event's dynamics.

Findings: The findings highlight how psychological tactics were used to exacerbate tensions and impact public perception of the rally.

These examples illustrate how psychological warfare tactics have been used by various actors, including the FBI, to create confusion, distrust, and division within targeted organizations. The associated documents and findings reveal the extent and impact of these tactics on social and political movements.

Recent cases involving psychological warfare tactics, such as threats, false information, and manipulation, often involve various governmental agencies, political groups, and media actors. Here are notable examples from the past decade:

Russian Interference in U.S. Elections (2016, 2020)

Incident: During the 2016 and 2020 U.S. presidential elections, Russian operatives employed psychological warfare to influence American voters.

Examples: Russian-backed disinformation campaigns used social media platforms to spread divisive and false narratives, create fake accounts, and manipulate public opinion.

Documents: The Mueller Report (2019) and subsequent intelligence community assessments detail these tactics. The Senate Intelligence Committee's report provides comprehensive analysis.

Findings: These tactics effectively sowed discord and influenced political discourse in the U.S., impacting public opinion and election outcomes.

COVID-19 Misinformation

Incident: During the COVID-19 pandemic, misinformation campaigns employed psychological tactics to create confusion and distrust about health measures and vaccines.

Examples: False information about the virus's origin, effectiveness of vaccines, and health guidelines was spread through social media and conspiracy theorist networks.

Documents: Research and reports from organizations like the WHO, CDC, and various fact-checking groups document the spread of misinformation. The U.S. Surgeon General's advisory on misinformation provides detailed examples.

Findings: These tactics led to increased public skepticism, vaccine hesitancy, and challenges in managing the pandemic effectively.

January 6 Capitol Riot (2021)

Incident: The January 6, 2021, Capitol riot involved psychological tactics aimed at inciting violence and creating confusion about election legitimacy.

Examples: Some participants spread false claims about election fraud and used provocateur tactics to escalate violence. Claims emerged that certain actions were orchestrated to discredit the broader anti-establishment movement.

Documents: Investigations by the FBI, the House Select Committee on the January 6 Attack, and various news outlets provide detailed accounts of these tactics.

Findings: The event led to heightened security measures, increased scrutiny of extremist groups, and a deeper investigation into psychological manipulation used to incite the riot.

Social Media Manipulation During Protests

Incident: During recent protests, such as those related to Black Lives Matter and climate change, there have been allegations of social media manipulation to create discord and undermine the movements.

Examples: False information and coordinated campaigns were used to discredit protests, create fake divisions, and spread confusion about protest goals and actions.

Documents: Reports by organizations like the Global Disinformation Index and various fact-checking services detail instances of manipulated social media content.

Findings: These efforts contributed to confusion and polarization, affecting the effectiveness and public perception of the protests.

Targeting of Political Figures and Activists

Incident: Recent political figures and activists have been targeted with psychological warfare tactics, including false information and threats.

Examples: Activists like Greta Thunberg and political figures like Alexandria Ocasio-Cortez have faced misinformation campaigns aimed at discrediting their work and creating public distrust.

Documents: Media reports and investigative journalism expose these campaigns. For instance, misinformation about Greta Thunberg's climate activism has been documented by various news outlets.

Findings: These tactics aim to undermine influential voices and influence public opinion on controversial issues.

Manipulation of Public Opinion on Immigration

Incident: Psychological tactics have been used to manipulate public opinion on immigration policies and debates.

Examples: Disinformation about immigration impacts, false claims about border security, and fear-based narratives have been spread to sway public opinion and create divisions.

Documents: Research by organizations like the Migration Policy Institute and reports from media watchdogs document these tactics.

Findings: These efforts contribute to polarized views on immigration and impact policy discussions and public sentiment.

Criteria for Psychological Warfare Tactics

Manipulation of Information: Use of false or misleading information to create confusion.

Creation of Division: Efforts to sow discord within groups or among the public.

Exploitation of Fear: Use of fear-based narratives to manipulate behavior and perceptions.

Coordination: Evidence of organized efforts behind psychological manipulation, such as coordinated disinformation campaigns.

These recent cases highlight how psychological warfare tactics are used to influence public perception, create confusion, and disrupt social and political processes. The documented findings reveal the extent and impact of these tactics on contemporary issues.

Several individuals and groups have been exposed for employing psychological warfare tactics, including the use of false information, manipulation, and threats. Here are specific examples of those who have been exposed in recent years:

Russian Operatives and Disinformation Campaigns

Individuals/Groups: The Internet Research Agency (IRA), associated with Russian intelligence services.

Exposure: Investigations by Robert Mueller's Special Counsel, the Senate Intelligence Committee, and various media reports.

Details: The IRA was found to be responsible for spreading misinformation, creating fake social media accounts, and manipulating public opinion in the U.S. around the 2016 and 2020 elections.

Right-Wing Media Figures and Platforms

Individuals/Groups: Figures like Alex Jones (InfoWars), and platforms such as Parler and Gab.

Exposure: Numerous fact-checking reports, investigations, and media analyses.

Details: These figures and platforms have been involved in spreading false information about COVID-19, the 2020 election, and other significant issues, contributing to public confusion and polarization.

Political Operatives and Groups

Individuals/Groups: Some operatives within political organizations and campaigns.

Exposure: Media investigations, whistleblower reports, and political analyses.

Details: Certain operatives have been exposed for using psychological tactics to manipulate public opinion, spread false narratives, or discredit political opponents. For instance, operatives involved in the Trump campaign were implicated in spreading misinformation and using psychological tactics during the 2016 election.

Conspiracy Theorists and Influencers

Individuals/Groups: Prominent conspiracy theorists like QAnon promoters.

Exposure: Investigations by journalists, fact-checkers, and social media platforms.

Details: Conspiracy theorists have been exposed for promoting unfounded theories and manipulating public perception on various issues, including election fraud and COVID-19.

Social Media Influencers and Bots

Individuals/Groups: Various influencers and automated bots.

Exposure: Reports from social media platforms (e.g., Facebook, Twitter) and research by organizations like Graphika.

Details: These actors have been found to spread false information and create divisive narratives by exploiting algorithms and user engagement patterns.

Government Agencies (in historical and some recent cases)

Individuals/Groups: Agencies like the FBI in historical contexts (COINTELPRO) and allegations of similar tactics in modern times.

Exposure: Historical records, declassified documents, and investigative journalism.

Details: While the historical COINTELPRO program is well-documented, recent allegations of psychological tactics by government agencies involve disinformation and manipulation, though direct evidence in recent cases is often less clear.

Corporate and Industry Interests

Individuals/Groups: Some corporations and industry groups.

Exposure: Investigative journalism and research by organizations like the Center for Media and Democracy.

Details: Corporations have been exposed for funding or promoting misinformation campaigns related to climate change, public health, and other issues to protect their interests.

Criteria for Exposure

Evidence of Manipulation: Clear documentation of tactics used to deceive or manipulate public opinion.

Investigative Reports: Findings from official investigations, journalistic inquiries, and fact-checking organizations.

Public Acknowledgment: Admission of tactics or strategies used by the individuals or groups involved.

These examples demonstrate how various individuals and groups have been exposed for employing psychological warfare tactics, contributing to the broader landscape of misinformation and manipulation in recent years.

High-Profile Cases of Coerced or False Confessions

1. The Central Park Five

Individuals: Kevin Richardson, Raymond Santana, Antron McCray, Yusef Salaam, Korey Wise

False Confession: In 1989, the five teenagers were coerced into confessing to the rape and assault of a white female jogger in Central Park. Their confessions were inconsistent and retracted.

Coercion: They were subjected to long, aggressive interrogations without legal representation. The police used threats and promises of leniency to obtain the confessions.

Responsible Parties: New York City Police Department detectives, including Detectives Steven Lopez, Michael Sheehan, and others.

Outcome: Their convictions were overturned in 2002 after DNA evidence and confessions from the actual perpetrator, Matias Reyes, proved their innocence.

The West Memphis Three

Individuals: Damien Echols, Jason Baldwin, Jessie Misskelley Jr.

False Confession: In 1993, Jessie Misskelley, who has an intellectual disability, was coerced into giving a false confession about his involvement in the murder of three eight-year-old boys in West Memphis, Arkansas.

Coercion: Misskelley was subjected to lengthy, unrecorded interrogations where he was misled about evidence and threatened with severe penalties.

Responsible Parties: Local police officers, including Detective Steve Jones and others.

Outcome: The three were released in 2011 after DNA evidence and public outcry revealed their innocence. They entered an Alford plea, maintaining their innocence but acknowledging sufficient evidence for conviction.

The Norfolk Four

Individuals: Danial Williams, Eric Wilson, Derrick, and George (not all directly coerced)

False Confession: In 1997, four men were coerced into confessing to the rape and murder of a woman in Norfolk, Virginia.

Coercion: The confessions were obtained through aggressive interrogation tactics, including threats and false promises of leniency.

Responsible Parties: Norfolk Police detectives, including Detective Charles "Chuck" Hardy and others.

Outcome: The confessions were discredited, and the actual perpetrator, Omar Ballard, was identified. The Norfolk Four were exonerated in 2009.

The Guildford Four

Individuals: Patrick Magee, Paul Hill, Gerry Conlon, Carole Richardson

False Confession: In the 1970s, the four were coerced into confessing to pub bombings in Guildford, England, which killed and injured several people.

Coercion: They were subjected to intense police interrogations, physical abuse, and threats.

Responsible Parties: British police officers, including those from the Metropolitan Police and the Surrey Police.

Outcome: Their convictions were overturned in 1989 after new evidence and a campaign by journalists and human rights organizations proved their innocence.

The Birmingham Six

Individuals: Patrick Hill, Gerard Hunter, William Power, Hugh Callaghan, Richard McIlkenny, Paddy Hill

False Confession: In 1974, the six were falsely convicted of conducting pub bombings in Birmingham, England, killing twenty-one people.

Coercion: The confessions were obtained under duress, including physical and psychological abuse.

Responsible Parties: British police officers involved in the investigation and interrogations.

Outcome: Their convictions were quashed in 1991 after it was proven they were innocent and had been wrongfully convicted due to police misconduct and fabricated evidence.

The Jena Six

Individuals: Six Black teenagers—Mychal Bell, Bobby Jindal, and others

False Confession: In 2006, the six teenagers were accused of assaulting a white student in Jena, Louisiana, after a series of racially charged incidents.

Coercion: Allegations emerged that the teens were coerced into confessing or that their confessions were used despite inconsistencies and lack of physical evidence.

Responsible Parties: Local law enforcement and prosecutors.

Outcome: The case gained national attention, leading to a reduction in charges and eventually dropped charges against some defendants. The case highlighted issues of racial bias and legal injustice.

The Richard Jewell Case

Individual: Richard Jewell

False Confession: Jewell was wrongfully accused of bombing Centennial Olympic Park during the 1996 Atlanta Olympics.

Coercion: Although not a confession, Jewell faced intense media scrutiny and FBI pressure, leading to him being wrongfully branded as a suspect.

Responsible Parties: FBI agents involved in the initial investigation, and media outlets like CNN that reported false information.

Outcome: Jewell was eventually exonerated, but the damage to his reputation was significant. The true bomber, Eric Robert Rudolph, was later apprehended.

Curtis Flowers

Case Overview: Convicted of a 1996 quadruple homicide in Mississippi. His convictions were overturned multiple times.

False Confession: Flowers initially confessed under intense interrogation, but his confession was inconsistent and later discredited.

Responsible Parties: Mississippi police officers and detectives, prosecutors relying on the flawed confession.

Joshua Schulte

Case Overview: A former CIA employee convicted for leaking classified documents. The initial confession was later retracted.

False Confession: Confession was made under duress and retracted. The defense argued it was influenced by improper interrogation methods.

Responsible Parties: FBI agents who used high-pressure tactics, prosecutors using the confession despite allegations of coercion.

Khalid A.

Case Overview: Accused of terrorism-related activities with a confession obtained under alleged coercion.

False Confession: Extracted through aggressive questioning and threats.

Responsible Parties: FBI agents who conducted the interrogation, those using manipulation tactics.

Jayland Walker

Case Overview: Involved in a high-profile police encounter. Confession was allegedly coerced.

False Confession: Influenced by coercive interrogation practices.

Responsible Parties: Akron police officers and investigators who used pressure tactics.

Robert Davis

Case Overview: Implicated in a Michigan robbery case with a confession obtained under questionable circumstances.

False Confession: Coerced through threats and deceptive interrogation techniques.

Responsible Parties: Police officers and detectives involved in the interrogation.

Kevin Cooper

Case Overview: Wrongfully convicted of the brutal murder of four people in California in 1983.

False Confession: Made under duress with inconsistencies emerging later.

Responsible Parties: Police officers and detectives using aggressive tactics and misleading information.

Richard Allen

Case Overview: Arrested in connection with a high-profile murder case in Indiana in 2023.

False Confession: Initially deemed questionable with inconsistencies.

Responsible Parties: Law enforcement officials and interrogators involved in the case.

These cases highlight the persistent issue of false confessions, and the significant role coercive interrogation practices play in wrongful convictions. They emphasize the need for reforms to protect individuals' rights and ensure justice.

The FBI, Media blackouts and manipulation

Here is a detailed look at the FBI's role in each of the cases where media blackouts or restrictions were involved:

The Assassination of Malcolm X

FBI Role:

The FBI was known to have monitored Malcolm X and other civil rights leaders under COINTELPRO.

The FBI had prior knowledge of threats to Malcolm X but did not act on them effectively.

The agency's role and any direct involvement or knowledge of the assassination were not fully investigated or reported until decades later.

Specific Actions:

Control over information: Limited details about the FBI's surveillance and involvement were released immediately after the assassination.

Influence on media: Early media coverage was shaped by limited information and FBI narratives.

The 1969 Chicago Police Raid

FBI Role:

The FBI engaged in monitoring and providing intelligence on the Black Panther Party, which contributed to the raid.

The Bureau's involvement was not officially known at the time of the raid.

Specific Actions:

Limited information release: The FBI's role and details about its informants were suppressed, influencing the initial media portrayal of the raid.

Narrative control: Early media reports framed the raid as a justified police action, minimizing the FBI's involvement.

The FBI and the Assassination of Martin Luther King Jr.

FBI Role:

The FBI surveyed Martin Luther King Jr. extensively as part of COINTELPRO.

There were efforts to undermine his reputation and disrupt his activities.

Specific Actions:

Suppression of information: Details about the FBI's surveillance and attempts to discredit King were not fully disclosed or investigated immediately after his assassination.

Media influence: The FBI's actions and the broader context of its surveillance were kept from public view for years.

The FBI and the 2013 Boston Marathon Bombing

FBI Role:

The FBI investigated the bombing, which involved Tamerlan and Dzhokhar Tsarnaev.

The Bureau exerted pressure on media outlets to control the narrative and prevent the spread of speculative or unverified information.

Specific Actions:

Media requests: The FBI requested media outlets to avoid discussing specific aspects of the investigation, including sensitive details about the suspects.

Information control: The FBI managed the flow of information to ensure the investigation's details were not compromised.

The FBI and the 2014 Ferguson Unrest

FBI Role:

The FBI engaged in monitoring and responding to the civil unrest in Ferguson following the police shooting of Michael Brown.

The Bureau played a role in managing public perception and media coverage of the unrest.

Specific Actions:

Restricting media access: There were reports of journalists facing detainment or harassment, which affected their ability to cover the protests freely.

Narrative management: The FBI influenced the narrative through press releases and controlled information flow.

The FBI and the Standing Rock Protests

FBI Role:

The FBI, along with other law enforcement agencies, monitored and responded to the protests against the Dakota Access Pipeline.

The Bureau's role included efforts to manage media coverage and suppress information about the protests.

Specific Actions:

Journalist restrictions: Reporters faced arrests and restrictions, limiting their ability to report on the protests and police response.

Influence on coverage: The FBI's actions contributed to limiting the public's understanding of the protests.

The FBI and the Snowden Revelations

FBI Role:

The FBI, along with other intelligence agencies, sought to suppress or manage the media coverage of Edward Snowden's leaks about NSA surveillance programs.

The Bureau participated in exerting pressure on media outlets and journalists to limit the spread of classified information.

Specific Actions:

Legal threats: The FBI and other agencies issued legal threats to media outlets, affecting how the Snowden revelations were reported.

Managing narrative: Efforts were made to control the narrative surrounding the leaks and limit the dissemination of sensitive details.

The FBI and the Whitmer Kidnapping Plot

FBI Role:

The FBI investigated a plot to kidnap Michigan Governor Gretchen Whitmer and arrested several individuals involved.

The Bureau managed the release of information and controlled media access to details about the investigation.

Specific Actions:

Information control: The FBI limited media access to the investigation details and shaped the narrative around domestic terrorism.

Media influence: Initial media reports were affected by the limited information provided by the FBI.

In each of these cases, the FBI's role involved controlling or influencing media coverage through various means, including information suppression, narrative management, and direct pressure on journalists and media outlets.

Psychological tactics examples

Here is the chronological list of the examples:

The FBI's Campaign Against Martin Luther King Jr. (1960s)

Public Perception: Blackmail attempts and disinformation campaigns aimed to undermine King's moral authority, affecting public views on his leadership.

Mistrust: Increased mistrust and paranoia among King's supporters and within the civil rights community.

COINTELPRO and the Black Panther Party (1960s-1970s)

Public Perception: Efforts to discredit the BPP portrayed them as violent and extremist, affecting public opinion due to manipulated media narratives.

Mistrust: Infiltration and false information led to internal mistrust within the BPP and among supporters, overshadowing legitimate civil rights efforts.

The Birmingham Six and Guildford Four Cases (1974-1991)

Public Perception: Psychological manipulation to obtain false confessions led to wrongful convictions, initially believed in by the public.

Mistrust: Once exposed, there was backlash against law enforcement and the legal system, leading to mistrust in their ability to deliver justice.

The FBI and the Anti-Globalization Movement (late 1990s-early 2000s)

Public Perception: Surveillance and misinformation distorted the view of anti-globalization protesters as violent or extreme.

Mistrust: Activists and the public became wary of law enforcement, fostering a sense of paranoia and distrust.

The FBI and the Occupy Wall Street Movement (2011)

Public Perception: FBI monitoring and controlled information contributed to the movement being viewed as disorganized or radical.

Mistrust: Distrust among protesters is due to perceived misrepresentation and suppression, affecting public perception and protest effectiveness.

The FBI and the 2014 Ferguson Unrest

Public Perception: Information control and journalist detainment led to a narrative focusing on violence and disorder rather than underlying racial issues.

Mistrust: Suppression of accurate reporting contributed to mistrust toward law enforcement and media, impacting how grievances were addressed.

The FBI and the Standing Rock Protests (2016)

Public Perception: Targeting of journalists and media control distorted the portrayal of the protests, focusing on clashes rather than core issues.

Mistrust: Increased mistrust toward law enforcement and government due to manipulated media coverage and actions against journalists.

The FBI and the Black Lives Matter Movement (2014-Present)

Public Perception: Surveillance, infiltration, and disinformation aimed at undermining the movement's effectiveness and public support.

Mistrust: Increased mistrust between activists and law enforcement, impacting efforts for reform and civil rights advancements.

The FBI and Anti-Immigration Activism (2010s-Present)

Public Perception: Surveillance and detainment of activists created a climate of fear and hindered immigration reform advocacy.

Mistrust: Fear and distrust among immigrant communities, affecting the effectiveness of advocacy and progress on civil rights.

Social Media Manipulation and Civil Rights (2010s-Present)

Public Perception: Use of misinformation and targeted ads distorted public opinion and affected civil rights issues.

Mistrust: Created deep divisions and mistrust in democratic processes and institutions, impacting advocacy effectiveness.

The FBI and COVID-19 Protests (2020-Present)

Public Perception: Surveillance and misinformation about lockdowns and vaccine mandates heightened polarization on public health measures.

Mistrust: Increased distrust in government authority and public health measures, influencing discussions on individual rights.

This list reflects the progression of psychological warfare tactics and their evolving impacts on civil rights and public perception.

COINTELPRO by any other Name

Current FBI tactics, while more sophisticated and technologically advanced, reflect some of the same objectives and strategies as COINTELPRO, though they are applied in a contemporary context. Here is how they align:

Surveillance and Monitoring

COINTELPRO: Involved extensive surveillance and infiltration of civil rights and activist groups to gather intelligence and disrupt their activities.

Current Tactics: Includes cyber surveillance, social media monitoring, and advanced technology to track and analyze potential threats. The focus remains on identifying and preemptively addressing perceived risks, though methods have evolved with technology.

Infiltration and Informants

COINTELPRO: Used undercover agents and informants to infiltrate groups, spread disinformation, and create internal conflicts.

Current Tactics: Involves infiltrating extremist groups and using informants to gather intelligence. Modern methods still aim to disrupt potential threats but rely on advanced techniques and digital tools.

Disinformation and Propaganda

COINTELPRO: Deployed disinformation to discredit and undermine targeted individuals and groups, creating mistrust and internal discord.

Current Tactics: Uses media management, public relations strategies, and sometimes misinformation to influence public perception and control narratives. The goal remains to manage how threats and groups are perceived by the public.

Community Relations and Outreach

COINTELPRO: Attempted to discredit and isolate civil rights groups, leading to a breakdown in community relations.

Current Tactics: Engages in community outreach to build trust and cooperation. However, the perception of the FBI's motivations and methods can still lead to skepticism and tension in some communities.

Counterintelligence and Disruption

COINTELPRO: Focused on disrupting and neutralizing perceived threats to national security through covert and often illegal methods.

Current Tactics: Continues to address threats through counterintelligence operations and initiative-taking measures. Modern techniques emphasize legality and coordination with other agencies, though concerns about overreach persist.

Use of Advanced Technology

COINTELPRO: Relied on less advanced surveillance methods and physical infiltration.

Current Tactics: Employs advanced technology such as facial recognition, data analytics, and digital forensics. The use of technology enhances investigative capabilities but raises new ethical and privacy concerns.

Legal and Ethical Concerns

COINTELPRO: Conducted operations that violated civil liberties and legal boundaries, leading to significant public and political backlash.

Current Tactics: Operates under legal frameworks and oversight but still faces scrutiny regarding privacy, civil liberties, and the balance between security and individual rights. There are ongoing debates about the ethical implications of current practices.

Impact on Public Perception and Trust

COINTELPRO: Undermined trust in law enforcement and created significant mistrust among targeted groups and the public.

Current Tactics: Efforts to control narratives and manage public perception can lead to similar mistrust and skepticism, especially if perceived as intrusive or biased.

Strategic Objectives

COINTELPRO: Aimed to neutralize and disrupt groups deemed threatening to national security or social order.

Current Tactics: Focus on preventing and responding to threats, maintaining national security, and managing public safety. The strategic goal of neutralizing perceived threats continues, but the approach has adapted to modern contexts.

Current FBI tactics reflect the same underlying objectives as COINTELPRO—addressing and neutralizing perceived threats to national security—though with updated methods and technology. While modern operations are intended to comply with legal standards and oversight, the fundamental strategies of surveillance, infiltration, and narrative control echo COINTELPRO's approach, leading to ongoing debates about their impact on civil liberties and public trust.

Legal Challanges

Current legal challenges related to FBI tactics and broader surveillance practices revolve around issues of privacy, civil liberties, and transparency. Here is a breakdown of these challenges:

1. Privacy Violations and Surveillance

Challenge: Increased surveillance capabilities, including the use of digital tools and social media monitoring, raise concerns about the erosion of privacy rights. The extensive collection of data on individuals without their consent can be seen as a violation of Fourth Amendment protections against unreasonable searches and seizures.

Legal Context: The Fourth Amendment and various state laws regulate the extent of surveillance and require warrants for certain types of searches and data collection. Courts frequently evaluate the legality of surveillance practices against these constitutional protections.

2. Informed Consent and Data Collection

Challenge: The FBI's use of digital surveillance often involves collecting vast amounts of data on individuals, including those not suspected of any crime. This can include data from social media, emails, and phone records.

Legal Context: Legal challenges focus on whether individuals have been adequately informed about the collection of their data and whether the FBI's methods comply with statutory requirements and judicial oversight. The use of Section 702 of the Foreign Intelligence Surveillance Act (FISA) and its implications for domestic surveillance are also debated.

3. Use of Informants and Entrapment

Challenge: The deployment of informants and undercover agents in various investigations can lead to claims of entrapment or coercion. There are concerns about whether informants provoke individuals to commit crimes they would not have otherwise engaged in.

Legal Context: Courts assess whether entrapment defenses are valid, considering whether law enforcement actions went beyond merely providing an opportunity to commit a crime. Entrapment claims are evaluated based on whether the government's conduct was excessive or induced criminal behavior.

4. Transparency and Accountability

Challenge: There is ongoing debate over the transparency of FBI operations, including how much information is shared with the public and oversight bodies. Lack of transparency can hinder accountability and public trust.

Legal Context: The Freedom of Information Act (FOIA) allows individuals to request information from federal agencies, including the FBI. Legal challenges often focus on the adequacy of responses to FOIA requests and whether agencies are withholding information improperly.

5. First Amendment Rights

Challenge: Surveillance and monitoring of political and social activists can raise concerns about infringement on First Amendment rights, including freedom of speech and assembly. There are concerns that such activities may stifle dissent and affect the ability of individuals to organize and protest.

Legal Context: Courts examine whether surveillance activities and other tactics violate First Amendment protections. There are ongoing discussions about balancing national security interests with the need to protect constitutional rights.

6. National Security vs. Civil Liberties

Challenge: The balance between national security and individual civil liberties is a recurring issue. The FBI's tactics are often justified on the grounds of protecting national security, but this can conflict with individual rights.

Legal Context: Legal frameworks, including the USA PATRIOT Act and the FISA Amendments Act, provide guidelines for balancing security measures with civil liberties. Courts and legislative bodies continually assess whether current laws and practices appropriately balance these interests.

7. Use of Artificial Intelligence and Technology

Challenge: The use of AI and advanced technology in surveillance and investigations raises questions about the legality and ethics of these methods. Issues include potential biases in algorithms and the accuracy of AI-driven assessments.

Legal Context: Legal challenges focus on the adequacy of regulations governing AI use and the potential for discrimination or privacy violations. Courts and regulatory bodies are exploring how existing laws apply to emerging technologies.

8. Handling of Sensitive Information

Challenge: The handling and potential mishandling of sensitive information, including classified data, can pose legal risks. There are concerns about whether information is securely protected and appropriately managed.

Legal Context: Legal standards for information security and classification are established by various laws and regulations. Challenges may involve evaluating whether these standards are met and addressing any breaches or improper handling.

9. Accountability for Misconduct

Challenge: Instances of misconduct, including illegal surveillance or abuse of power, necessitate accountability. There are concerns about whether appropriate measures are in place to address and rectify such issues.

Legal Context: Oversight mechanisms, including congressional committees and inspector general reports, play a role in addressing allegations of misconduct. Legal challenges may involve holding agencies accountable for any violations and ensuring effective remedies are in place.

10. Impact of Emerging Threats

Challenge: The evolving nature of threats, including cyber threats and domestic extremism, complicates the legal landscape. The FBI must navigate how to address these threats while adhering to legal and ethical standards.

Legal Context: Legal responses to emerging threats involve adapting existing laws and creating new regulations. Courts and policymakers work to address how best to manage these challenges without compromising civil liberties.

Here are some notable recent legal cases and issues related to the FBI and broader surveillance and civil liberties concerns:

1. United States v. Michael Sussmann (2022)

Case Summary: Michael Sussmann, a cybersecurity lawyer, was charged with making a false statement to the FBI during the investigation into the Trump-Russia allegations. The case focused on whether Sussmann misled the FBI about his representation of clients.

Legal Significance: The case highlighted issues around the accuracy of information provided to federal agencies and the potential consequences of misleading statements. It also raised questions about the role of legal representation and the limits of prosecuting false statements to law enforcement.

2. USA v. Edward Snowden (2013-Present)

Case Summary: Edward Snowden, a former NSA contractor, leaked classified information revealing widespread government surveillance programs. He faces charges under the Espionage Act for his disclosures.

Legal Significance: Snowden's case has sparked extensive debate about whistleblowing, government surveillance, and privacy rights. The case has implications for how whistleblowers are treated and the balance between national security and civil liberties.

3. ACLU v. FBI (2019-Present)

Case Summary: The American Civil Liberties Union (ACLU) has been involved in ongoing litigation against the FBI over its surveillance practices, including the use of National Security Letters (NSLs) and other data collection methods.

Legal Significance: This case focuses on the transparency and legality of the FBI's surveillance techniques and the impact on privacy rights. The litigation challenges the scope and oversight of surveillance practices under existing laws.

4. MedeAnalytics v. FBI (2020-Present)

Case Summary: MedeAnalytics, a data analytics company, challenged the FBI's use of its data collection practices. The company argued that its data was collected without proper legal authority and in violation of privacy protections.

Legal Significance: This case deals with the legality of data collection from private entities and raises questions about the boundaries of government access to personal data.

5. Barton v. U.S. Department of Justice (2021)

Case Summary: This case involved a challenge to the FBI's handling of data collected during investigations, including allegations of improper data use and retention.

Legal Significance: It highlights concerns about how government agencies manage and protect sensitive data and the legal standards governing data retention and privacy.

6. First Unitarian Church of Los Angeles v. NSA (2022)

Case Summary: The First Unitarian Church of Los Angeles sued the NSA, alleging that its members were subjected to illegal surveillance. The case questioned the legality and scope of surveillance on religious and political groups.

Legal Significance: The case addresses the intersection of religious freedoms and surveillance, focusing on the legal limits of monitoring religious and political groups.

7. Privacy Rights Clearinghouse v. FBI (2022)

Case Summary: Privacy Rights Clearinghouse challenged the FBI's practices related to the collection and handling of personal data. The case examined whether the FBI's data collection methods complied with privacy laws.

Legal Significance: This case emphasizes the ongoing debate over privacy rights and the adequacy of legal protections against government data collection practices.

8. Doe v. FBI (2021)

Case Summary: Anonymous plaintiffs sued the FBI for alleged violations of privacy and civil liberties, including unwarranted surveillance and data collection.

Legal Significance: The case addresses concerns about the scope of government surveillance and the protection of individual rights under the Constitution.

9. Klayman v. Obama (2015-Present)

Case Summary: Larry Klayman, a conservative activist, challenged the constitutionality of the NSA's bulk data collection programs. The case has implications for the legality of surveillance practices and privacy rights.

Legal Significance: The case explores the boundaries of government surveillance and the impact on Fourth Amendment rights. It reflects ongoing concerns about the balance between security and privacy.

10. United States v. Julian Assange (2019-Present)

Case Summary: Julian Assange, the founder of WikiLeaks, faces extradition to the U.S. on charges related to the publication of classified documents. The case involves charges under the Espionage Act and raises issues about press freedom and government secrecy.

Legal Significance: The case has implications for press freedoms and the treatment of whistleblowers, impacting how government secrets and leaks are managed legally.

These recent legal cases highlight ongoing tensions between government surveillance, privacy rights, and civil liberties. They reflect broader debates about the scope of government power, the protection of individual rights, and the balance between national security and personal freedoms.

Domestic Operations

Several domestic operations and programs in the U.S. have been publicly acknowledged or suspected to involve tactics similar to those used in more recent controversies. These operations often involve surveillance, infiltration, and psychological tactics. Here are some notable examples:

1. Operation CHAOS (1967-1974)

Overview: Operation CHAOS was a covert CIA program aimed at monitoring and infiltrating anti-war and civil rights groups in the U.S. The goal was to understand and counter the influence of foreign entities on domestic dissent.

Tactics: The operation used surveillance, infiltration, and psychological tactics to gather intelligence and influence public opinion.

Similarity: Like COINTELPRO, Operation CHAOS involved extensive surveillance and manipulation of domestic groups. Both programs targeted dissenting voices and sought to undermine their effectiveness.

2. Operation Gladio (Post-World War II)

Overview: Operation Gladio was a covert NATO operation involving secret armies in Europe to counter Soviet influence. While primarily European, similar tactics were allegedly used domestically.

Tactics: The operation involved clandestine activities, including false flag operations and psychological manipulation.

Similarity: The covert nature of Operation Gladio and its psychological operations are reminiscent of COINTELPRO's efforts to control and influence public perception and domestic political movements.

3. Operation Northwoods (1962)

Overview: Operation Northwoods was a proposed plan by the U.S. Department of Defense for false-flag operations to justify military action against Cuba. Although never implemented, it involved creating fabricated incidents to influence public opinion.

Tactics: The plan included ideas for psychological operations and misinformation to manipulate public perception.

Similarity: The use of psychological manipulation to influence public opinion mirrors the tactics used in COINTELPRO and other covert operations.

4. Operation Snow White (1970s)

Overview: Operation Snow White was a covert operation by the Church of Scientology to infiltrate and steal documents from government agencies, including the IRS, to suppress criticism.

Tactics: The operation involved espionage, infiltration, and manipulation to influence government actions and public perception.

Similarity: The infiltration and manipulation tactics used in Operation Snow White are similar to those employed in COINTELPRO to undermine targeted groups and individuals.

5. The NSA's "Stellarwind" (2001-Present)

Overview: Stellarwind is a classified NSA program involving the interception of communications without warrants, part of broader post-9/11 surveillance efforts.

Tactics: The program includes extensive data collection and surveillance, often criticized for violating privacy rights.

Similarity: Like COINTELPRO, Stellarwind involves extensive surveillance and data collection, raising concerns about civil liberties and government overreach.

6. The FBI's "Operation Crossfire Hurricane" (2016-2019)

Overview: Operation Crossfire Hurricane was the FBI's investigation into Russian interference in the 2016 U.S. presidential election. It involved surveillance of individuals connected to the Trump campaign.

Tactics: The operation used extensive surveillance and intelligence gathering, similar to COINTELPRO's methods.

Similarity: The investigation's tactics, including surveillance and the monitoring of political figures, echo COINTELPRO's approach to handling perceived threats to national security.

7. FBI's Surveillance of Environmental and Animal Rights Activists (2000s-Present)

Overview: The FBI has monitored and investigated environmental and animal rights activists, labeling some as "domestic extremists" and using surveillance and infiltration.

Tactics: These tactics involve surveillance, infiltration, and efforts to discredit and disrupt activist activities.

Similarity: The focus on surveillance and psychological tactics to undermine activist groups is reminiscent of COINTELPRO's approach to dealing with civil rights and political organizations.

8. FBI's Monitoring of Muslim Americans (Post-9/11)

Overview: In the wake of 9/11, the FBI engaged in surveillance and infiltration of Muslim communities and organizations as part of counter-terrorism efforts.

Tactics: The program involved surveillance, informant recruitment, and community monitoring.

Similarity: The tactics used in monitoring Muslim Americans reflect the surveillance and infiltration methods similar to those employed in COINTELPRO.

These operations and programs share similarities with COINTELPRO in their use of covert surveillance, psychological manipulation, and efforts to undermine or disrupt targeted groups. They reflect ongoing concerns about government overreach, civil liberties, and the balance between national security and individual rights.

Recent U.S. domestic operations and activities that show parallels to COINTELPRO reflect the continuation of covert surveillance, psychological manipulation, and efforts to undermine dissenting groups. Here are some notable recent examples:

FBI's Surveillance of Black Lives Matter (BLM) Movement (2014-Present)

Overview: The FBI has been involved in monitoring and investigating the Black Lives Matter movement, which advocates for racial justice and police reform.

Tactics: Surveillance, infiltration, and information leaks have been reported. There have been claims of the FBI attempting to create divisions within the movement and to discredit its leaders.

Parallels to COINTELPRO: Similar to COINTELPRO's efforts to undermine the Black Panther Party and other civil rights groups, these tactics aim to disrupt and discredit a prominent social justice movement.

FBI's Monitoring of Anti-Immigration Activism (2010s-Present)

Overview: Activists advocating for immigrant rights have been subject to surveillance and infiltration by the FBI, particularly those involved in protests or advocacy against immigration policies.

Tactics: Includes surveillance, infiltration, and leaks to discredit activists.

Parallels to COINTELPRO: Reflects COINTELPRO's use of surveillance and psychological tactics to disrupt and undermine advocacy efforts, similar to the targeting of civil rights and anti-war activists in the 1960s.

FBI and the Standing Rock Protests (2016)

Overview: The Standing Rock protests against the Dakota Access Pipeline saw significant law enforcement and FBI involvement.

Tactics: Surveillance, infiltration, and efforts to control media narratives. There were also reports of aggressive tactics to suppress protest activities.

Parallels to COINTELPRO: Similar to COINTELPRO's targeting of activist groups like AIM, the tactics used aimed to disrupt and discredit protest movements critical of government and corporate interests.

FBI's Actions During the 2020 Black Lives Matter Protests

Overview: During the widespread protests following George Floyd's death, the FBI engaged in monitoring and managing the narrative surrounding the protests.

Tactics: Control of media narratives, surveillance of activists, and dissemination of misinformation.

Parallels to COINTELPRO: Efforts to manage public perception and undermine the effectiveness of the protests are reminiscent of COINTELPRO's tactics to disrupt and discredit civil rights movements.

Social Media Manipulation and Misinformation Campaigns (2010s-Present)

Overview: Psychological operations and misinformation campaigns have been used to influence public opinion and create divisions on social media platforms.

Tactics: Includes the use of bots, fake accounts, and targeted ads to spread disinformation and influence social and political issues.

Parallels to COINTELPRO: The manipulation of public opinion and creation of divisions mirrors COINTELPRO's efforts to control narratives and disrupt activist and political groups.

FBI's Surveillance of Environmental and Animal Rights Activists (2000s-Present)

Overview: Environmental and animal rights activists have faced surveillance and infiltration by the FBI, with some being labeled as domestic extremists.

Tactics: Surveillance, infiltration, and attempts to discredit or disrupt activism.

Parallels to COINTELPRO: Reflects COINTELPRO's approach of surveilling and undermining groups seen as a threat to government or corporate interests.

FBI's Monitoring of Muslim American Communities (Post-9/11)

Overview: Post-9/11 surveillance has targeted Muslim American communities and organizations, focusing on counter-terrorism efforts.

Tactics: Surveillance, informant recruitment, and community monitoring.

Parallels to COINTELPRO: The focus on surveillance and infiltration of a specific community is similar to COINTELPRO's targeting of civil rights and political activists.

Recent Investigations into Far-Right Extremist Groups (2010s-Present)

Overview: The FBI has investigated far-right extremist groups involved in violent activities and domestic terrorism.

Tactics: Infiltration, surveillance, and monitoring of communications.

Summary

These recent examples reflect ongoing practices that are reminiscent of COINTELPRO's methods, including surveillance, psychological tactics, and efforts to disrupt and discredit targeted groups. They highlight a continuing debate about the balance between national security and civil liberties, and the impact of such practices on public trust and civil rights.

recent examples of U.S. domestic operations that exhibit similarities to COINTELPRO's tactics, Liberal

1. FBI and Anti-Vaccine Activists (2010s-Present)

Overview: The FBI has monitored and investigated anti-vaccine activists, particularly those involved in large-scale protests or campaigns against vaccination policies.

Tactics: Surveillance, infiltration, and attempts to discredit activists through media leaks and misinformation.

Parallels to COINTELPRO: Similar to COINTELPRO's efforts to disrupt civil rights and anti-war groups, these tactics aim to undermine the credibility of activists and influence public perception.

2. FBI's Surveillance of Protest Movements Against Police Brutality (2010s-Present)

Overview: Various protest movements advocating against police brutality and systemic racism have been subject to FBI monitoring.

Tactics: Includes surveillance of organizers, infiltration of groups, and manipulation of media coverage to portray these movements as radical or violent.

Parallels to COINTELPRO: Echoes COINTELPRO's strategies to discredit and fragment civil rights organizations by creating internal strife and manipulating public narratives.

3. FBI and Digital Activism (2010s-Present)

Overview: The FBI has targeted digital activists and online movements, including those advocating for various social and political causes.

Tactics: Monitoring social media activity, infiltration of online groups, and spreading disinformation to influence public opinion and disrupt activist efforts.

Parallels to COINTELPRO: Reflects COINTELPRO's use of psychological operations and misinformation to control narratives and discredit movements.

4. FBI's Role in the January 6 Capitol Riot Investigation (2020-Present)

Overview: The FBI's investigation into the January 6, 2020, Capitol riot has involved extensive surveillance and monitoring of far-right extremist groups.

Tactics: Use of informants, infiltration of extremist groups, and selective leaks of information to shape public perception of the riot and its participants.

Parallels to COINTELPRO: Similar to COINTELPRO's infiltration and manipulation tactics, these actions aim to control the narrative and manage public perception of extremist groups.

5. FBI and Environmental Activist Groups (2020s)

Overview: The FBI has monitored environmental activist groups involved in protests against climate change policies and industrial activities.

Tactics: Surveillance, infiltration, and attempts to discredit activists through misinformation and media manipulation.

Parallels to COINTELPRO: These tactics mirror COINTELPRO's efforts to disrupt and undermine environmental and anti-war movements by targeting their organization and public image.

6. FBI's Monitoring of Social Justice Activists (2020s)

Overview: Social justice activists involved in various causes, including gender equality and racial justice, have faced FBI surveillance and infiltration.

Tactics: Infiltration of activist groups, surveillance, and dissemination of misleading information to create divisions and diminish the effectiveness of advocacy efforts.

Parallels to COINTELPRO: Echoes COINTELPRO's approach of surveilling and manipulating activist groups to control their influence and impact.

7. FBI and Anti-Government Extremist Groups (2010s-Present)

Overview: The FBI has targeted anti-government extremist groups, including militias and sovereign citizen movements, involved in violent or illegal activities.

Tactics: Surveillance, infiltration, and the use of informants to gather intelligence and disrupt these groups' activities.

Parallels to COINTELPRO: The approach mirrors COINTELPRO's tactics of using infiltration and psychological manipulation to control and disrupt perceived threats.

8. FBI and Left-Wing Activists (2020s)

Overview: The FBI has targeted left-wing activist groups involved in protests against economic inequality and corporate power.

Tactics: Surveillance, infiltration, and efforts to discredit activists through misinformation and controlled media narratives.

Parallels to COINTELPRO: Similar to COINTELPRO's methods used against leftist and radical groups, these tactics aim to undermine and discredit activism.

9. FBI and Grassroots Organizing Groups (2020s)

Overview: The FBI has monitored grassroots organizing efforts aimed at various social justice issues, including housing and labor rights.

Tactics: Surveillance, infiltration, and attempts to discredit grassroots organizations and their leaders.

Parallels to COINTELPRO: Reflects COINTELPRO's tactics of targeting grassroots and activist organizations to weaken their influence and public support.

Summary

These additional examples illustrate how modern surveillance and psychological tactics used by agencies like the FBI share similarities with COINTELPRO's methods. The ongoing use of covert operations, disinformation, and infiltration reflects a continuity of strategies aimed at controlling and discrediting dissenting voices and movements.

list of U.S. domestic operations involving conservative groups, ranked by the most tactics used:

1. FBI and Militia Groups (2010s-Present)

Tactics: Infiltration, surveillance, use of informants, intelligence gathering, and disruption.

Overview: Various militia groups with anti-government ideologies have been targeted by the FBI for their perceived threats.

2. FBI and Proud Boys (2010s-Present)

Tactics: Surveillance, infiltration, use of informants, intelligence gathering, and disruption.

Overview: The Proud Boys, involved in violent confrontations and extremist activities, have been subject to extensive monitoring.

3. FBI and Oath Keepers (2010s-Present)

Tactics: Surveillance, infiltration, use of informants, intelligence gathering, and disruption.

Overview: The Oath Keepers, a far-right militia group, have been heavily monitored due to their anti-government stance.

4. FBI and Three Percenters (2010s-Present)

Tactics: Infiltration, surveillance, intelligence gathering, and disruption.

Overview: The Three Percenters, another right-wing militia group, have been investigated for their anti-government views.

5. FBI and "Boogaloo" Movement (2010s-Present)

Tactics: Surveillance, infiltration, use of informants, intelligence gathering, and disruption.

Overview: The "Boogaloo" movement, advocating for a second civil war, has been closely monitored due to its extremist rhetoric.

6. FBI and QAnon Supporters (2010s-Present)

Tactics: Surveillance, infiltration, use of informants, and intelligence gathering.

Overview: QAnon supporters have been monitored for their involvement in extremist activities and conspiracy theories.

7. FBI and Anti-Government Protesters (2010s-Present)

Tactics: Surveillance, infiltration, and disruption.

Overview: Anti-government movements with conservative or libertarian tendencies have faced FBI scrutiny.

8. FBI and Tea Party Activists (2009-2010s)

Tactics: Surveillance and intelligence gathering.

Overview: The Tea Party movement, associated with conservative and anti-tax sentiments, was monitored during its rise.

9. FBI and Christian Identity Movement (1990s-Present)

Tactics: Surveillance and infiltration.

Overview: The Christian Identity movement, a far-right religious group, has been monitored for potential links to violence.

10. FBI and Anti-Abortion Extremist Groups (2010s-Present)

Tactics: Surveillance, infiltration, and intelligence gathering.

Overview: Extremist anti-abortion groups involved in violent activities have been investigated by the FBI.

11. FBI and Traditionalist Workers Party (2010s-Present)

Tactics: Surveillance, infiltration, and intelligence gathering.

Overview: The Traditionalist Workers Party, known for its white nationalist views, has been targeted for its extremist agenda.

12. FBI and Patriot Prayer (2010s-Present)

Tactics: Surveillance and intelligence gathering.

Overview: Patriot Prayer, involved in violent confrontations with leftist groups, has been monitored by the FBI.

13. FBI and American Renaissance (2010s-Present)

Tactics: Surveillance, infiltration, and intelligence gathering.

Overview: American Renaissance, a white nationalist organization, has been subject to FBI monitoring for its extremist activities.

This ranking reflects the extent and variety of tactics used by the FBI in monitoring and managing these conservative groups, highlighting parallels to COINTELPRO's methods.

Parallels to COINTELPRO: Similar to COINTELPRO's tactics of monitoring and manipulating groups perceived as radical or disruptive, aiming to control their influence and impact.

These examples illustrate how contemporary operations against conservative and right-wing groups utilize tactics reminiscent of COINTELPRO. Infiltration, surveillance, and disinformation are used to manage and disrupt perceived threats, similar to the methods employed during the COINTELPRO era. The continuation of such tactics reflects ongoing concerns about political and ideological movements deemed as threats by law enforcement agencies.

Government Response to criticism

Government responses to criticism regarding surveillance and monitoring of domestic groups often involve several strategies and statements. These responses generally focus on justifying actions, emphasizing legal and ethical frameworks, and addressing specific concerns raised by critics. Here is a detailed look at how the government typically responds:

1. Justification of Actions

National Security: Government officials often emphasize that surveillance and monitoring are necessary for national security. They argue that these measures are essential for preventing domestic terrorism and violent extremism.

Legal Authority: Officials assert that their actions are authorized under laws such as the USA PATRIOT Act, the Foreign Intelligence

Surveillance Act (FISA), and other statutes that grant broad surveillance powers to agencies like the FBI and DHS.

2. Legal and Oversight Framework

Checks and Balances: Government responses highlight the legal and procedural safeguards in place to prevent abuse. This includes oversight by courts (e.g., the Foreign Intelligence Surveillance Court), congressional committees, and internal agency watchdogs.

Transparency and Accountability: Agencies may point to their efforts to increase transparency and accountability, such as reporting to Congress or public disclosures of certain operations.

3. Addressing Specific Criticisms

Infiltration and Entrapment Concerns: When criticized for infiltrating groups or using informants, the government may argue that these tactics are necessary to prevent violence and that they are used in accordance with established protocols.

Impact on Civil Liberties: In response to concerns about civil liberties and constitutional rights, officials may argue that their actions are proportionate and targeted, aiming to minimize unnecessary impact on innocent individuals.

4. Public Relations and Media

Media Statements: Government representatives frequently provide statements to the media to clarify and justify their actions. These statements often focus on the effectiveness of surveillance in preventing threats and ensuring public safety.

Public Engagement: Occasionally, government agencies engage in public forums or issue reports to explain their policies and operations, aiming to build public trust and understanding.

5. Legislative and Policy Reforms

Policy Adjustments: In response to criticism, there may be calls for legislative or policy reforms. This can include efforts to revise surveillance guidelines, enhance oversight mechanisms, or improve transparency.

Bipartisan Efforts: Sometimes, criticism leads to bipartisan efforts to address concerns, resulting in new regulations or amendments to existing laws to better balance security and civil liberties.

6. Denials of Wrongdoing

Rebuttals to Allegations: Government officials may deny allegations of misconduct or overreach, arguing that any perceived excesses are either isolated incidents or misunderstandings of their operational protocols.

7. Advocacy for Support

Public Support: Government agencies may seek to bolster public support for their activities by emphasizing the threats they are addressing and the successes of their operations in maintaining national security.

8. Addressing Specific Incidents

Case-by-Case Responses: In cases where specific incidents of surveillance or monitoring come under scrutiny, officials may provide detailed explanations or defenses related to those particular cases, often highlighting the context and legal justifications.

These responses are designed to reassure the public and stakeholders that government surveillance and monitoring are conducted within legal bounds and with appropriate oversight, while also addressing specific criticisms and concerns raised by various groups and individuals.

Government overreach evidence

Evidence of government overreach can manifest in numerous ways, often involving the violation of privacy rights, abuse of surveillance powers, or excessive intrusion into personal and political activities. Here are some key indicators and examples of government overreach, particularly related to surveillance and monitoring:

1. Abuse of Surveillance Powers:

Unjustified Surveillance: Cases where individuals or groups are monitored without clear, justified reasons or probable cause. This includes situations where surveillance is conducted on political activists or groups without evidence of criminal activity.

Overbroad Surveillance: Instances where surveillance is excessively broad or indiscriminate, capturing data from a large number of people who are not targets of investigation.

2. Infringement on Civil Liberties:

Violation of Privacy: Evidence that surveillance or data collection infringes on individuals' rights to privacy as protected by the Fourth Amendment. This includes unauthorized access to private communications, financial records, or personal information.

Chilling Effect on Free Speech: Instances where government surveillance or monitoring leads to self-censorship or suppression of political and free speech, creating a chilling effect on public discourse and activism.

3. Historical and Recent Examples:

COINTELPRO (1956-1971): The FBI's COINTELPRO program involved widespread illegal surveillance and infiltration of civil rights groups, political organizations, and activists, often using methods such as misinformation, harassment, and illegal wiretaps.

NSA Surveillance Controversies: Revelations from Edward Snowden in 2013 exposed the NSA's extensive data collection programs, including bulk collection of telephone metadata and internet communications, raising concerns about violations of privacy rights and the Fourth Amendment.

FBI's Monitoring of Political Activists: Reports of the FBI monitoring and infiltrating political groups, including some conservative and far-right movements, where the surveillance or infiltration seems disproportionate to any actual threat posed by these groups.

4. Legal Challenges and Court Rulings:

Judicial Findings: Court cases that have ruled against government agencies for overreach, such as decisions that found violations of privacy rights or improper use of surveillance powers. For example, the Supreme Court has occasionally ruled against practices deemed unconstitutional or exceeding legal boundaries.

Settlement Agreements: Cases where the government has settled lawsuits related to overreach, often involving agreements to alter practices, pay damages, or implement reforms.

5. Whistleblower Revelations:

Insider Reports: Testimonies from whistleblowers within government agencies that reveal instances of illegal or unethical surveillance practices. These accounts often provide detailed insights into abuses of power and overreach.

6. Public and Media Reports:

Investigative Journalism: Reports by journalists and media organizations that expose instances of government overreach, including illegal surveillance, abuse of power, and violations of civil liberties.

Government Accountability Reports: Findings from watchdog organizations and independent audits that highlight instances of overreach and recommend reforms or corrective actions.

7. Policy and Oversight Failures:

Lack of Oversight: Situations where there is inadequate oversight or accountability for surveillance practices, leading to unchecked power and potential abuses.

Policy Violations: Instances where government agencies violate their own policies or legal requirements regarding surveillance, such as failing to obtain proper warrants or exceeding authorized surveillance limits.

These indicators and examples collectively illustrate the ways in which government overreach can occur, often involving significant concerns about privacy, civil liberties, and the balance of power between state authorities and individual rights.

free speech impacted

Free speech in the United States has been impacted by a range of factors related to government actions, societal changes, and technological advancements. Here are some key ways in which free speech has been affected:

1. Surveillance and Monitoring:

Chilling Effect: Government surveillance and monitoring, especially when broad and indiscriminate, can lead to a chilling effect on free speech. People may self-censor or avoid discussing controversial topics out of fear that their communications are being monitored.

Targeted Monitoring: Specific targeting of individuals or groups based on their speech or activism can suppress dissent and discourage public participation in political and social discourse.

2. Content Moderation and Censorship:

Social Media Platforms: Private companies, including social media platforms, play a significant role in moderating content. While they are not government entities, their content policies can impact free speech by removing or restricting posts deemed to violate their terms of service.

Government Influence: There have been concerns about government influence on or pressure applied to social media platforms to remove certain types of content, which can blur the line between private and public censorship.

3. Legislative and Policy Measures:

Anti-Terrorism Laws: Post-9/11 anti-terrorism laws, such as the PATRIOT Act, expanded surveillance and investigative powers, which some argue have infringed on privacy rights and free speech by allowing for increased monitoring of communications and activities.

Hate Speech Laws: Legislation aimed at curbing hate speech can sometimes lead to debates about the limits of free speech and the balance between protecting individuals from harm and preserving free expression.

4. Legal Cases and Precedents:

Court Rulings: Legal cases that address the limits of free speech, such as those involving obscenity, defamation, or national security, shape the boundaries of protected speech. For instance, the Supreme Court has ruled on various cases balancing free speech with other interests, such as in Brandenburg v. Ohio (1969), which established the "imminent lawless action" standard for speech.

Free Speech Zones: The creation of "free speech zones" at public events or protests, where dissenting voices are confined to specific areas, can be seen as a restriction on the free expression of ideas in public spaces.

5. Public and Private Sector Actions:

Corporate Policies: Companies and organizations may impose their own restrictions on speech through codes of conduct, employee handbooks, and public statements, impacting the ability of individuals to express themselves freely in the workplace or in association with these entities.

Academic Institutions: Controversies over campus speech and the role of academic institutions in regulating or restricting speech can influence the discourse around free speech in educational settings.

6. Societal and Cultural Trends:

Political Polarization: Increasing political polarization can affect free speech by creating environments where certain viewpoints are heavily scrutinized or attacked, potentially leading to a more hostile atmosphere for open discourse.

Public Shaming and Online Harassment: The rise of online shaming and harassment can lead to self-censorship and suppression of dissenting or controversial viewpoints out of fear of backlash or personal harm.

7. Whistleblower and Leak Cases:

Legal Actions Against Whistleblowers: Legal actions against whistleblowers who expose government or corporate misconduct can have a chilling effect on free speech by discouraging individuals from speaking out about issues of public concern.

Leak Investigations: Investigations into leaks and unauthorized disclosures can impact journalistic freedom and the ability to report on sensitive topics.

8. State and Local Government Actions:

Restrictive Legislation: Some state and local governments have enacted laws or policies that restrict speech, particularly related to protests, assembly, and public demonstrations. These measures can limit the ability of individuals to engage in free expression.

These factors collectively demonstrate how free speech in the U.S. is impacted by a combination of government actions, societal changes, and technological developments. The balance between maintaining security and protecting individual freedoms continues to be a central issue in discussions about free speech and its limitations.

First Amendment threats

The First Amendment, which guarantees freedoms of speech, press, assembly, and religion, faces a variety of threats in contemporary society. These threats come from both governmental actions and societal pressures. Here are some of the key threats to First Amendment rights:

1. Government Surveillance and Censorship:

Surveillance: Increased surveillance by government agencies, particularly under laws like the PATRIOT Act, can lead to a chilling effect on free speech, where individuals may self-censor due to fear of being monitored.

Content Regulation: Government attempts to regulate or censor online content, often under the guise of national security or combating misinformation, can infringe on free speech rights.

2. Anti-Terrorism and National Security Measures:

Broad Definitions: Anti-terrorism laws can sometimes include broad definitions of "terrorist activities" that might encroach on legitimate forms of political expression and dissent.

Preemptive Actions: Actions taken to prevent potential threats can sometimes overreach, restricting speech, and assembly rights under the justification of preventing violence or terrorism.

3. Corporate and Platform Censorship:

Content Moderation: Social media platforms and other private entities have significant control over what content is allowed on their platforms, which can lead to censorship of certain viewpoints.

Corporate Policies: Companies can impose their own restrictions on speech, affecting employees' ability to express their views both in and out of the workplace.

4. Legislation and Legal Restrictions:

Hate Speech Laws: Some laws aimed at preventing hate speech may inadvertently restrict free speech by setting limits on what can be expressed publicly.

Public Speech Zones: Restrictions on where protests and public speeches can occur, such as "free speech zones," may limit the effectiveness and reach of expressive activities.

5. Social and Cultural Pressures:

Political Correctness: Pressure to conform to social norms or political correctness can stifle open debate and discourage the expression of dissenting or controversial opinions.

Public Shaming and Cancel Culture: Social and public pressure can lead to self-censorship and discourage individuals from expressing unpopular or controversial opinions due to fear of backlash.

6. Threats to the Press:

Journalist Protection: Investigations and prosecutions against journalists and whistleblowers can deter reporting on prominent issues and limit press freedom.

Media Consolidation: The concentration of media ownership can reduce the diversity of viewpoints and impact the quality and scope of news coverage.

7. Criminalization of Speech:

Anti-Protest Laws: Laws targeting specific forms of protest or dissent, such as anti-riot laws or legislation aimed at disrupting protests, can infringe upon assembly and speech rights.

Defamation and Libel Laws: Aggressive use of defamation and libel lawsuits can be used to suppress criticism and discourage public discourse.

8. Internet and Technology Issues:

Data Privacy Concerns: Data collection and privacy issues related to online activity can make individuals wary of expressing themselves freely on digital platforms.

Algorithmic Censorship: Algorithms used by tech companies to filter content can inadvertently suppress legitimate speech and limit the diversity of information available.

9. Restrictions on Academic Freedom:

Campus Speech Codes: Some universities have implemented speech codes or policies that restrict controversial or unpopular viewpoints, impacting academic freedom and debate.

Political Influence: Political pressures on academic institutions can influence research and teaching, potentially limiting scholarly inquiry and expression.

10. Impact of Polarization:

Echo Chambers: Increased political and social polarization can create echo chambers where only certain viewpoints are amplified, potentially leading to suppression of opposing views.

Intimidation and Harassment: Individuals expressing controversial opinions may face intimidation or harassment, leading to self-censorship and limiting open debate.

These threats reflect ongoing challenges to First Amendment protections, highlighting the need for vigilance and advocacy to ensure that free speech and other fundamental rights are preserved in a rapidly evolving landscape.

recent polarizing events

Polarization in recent years has intensified due to a combination of factors, including political, social, and technological influences. While the FBI and CIA have not explicitly manipulated events to increase polarization, there have been instances where their actions, as well as broader government and external influences, have contributed to divisive narratives. Here is a look at how polarization has worsened and some key events that have played a role:

Factors Contributing to Increased Polarization:

Social Media and Digital Echo Chambers:

Algorithmic Amplification: Social media algorithms often prioritize sensational and emotionally charged content, reinforcing existing biases and creating echo chambers.

Misinformation and Disinformation: The spread of false or misleading information, often through social media, exacerbates divisions and fosters distrust.

Political Polarization:

Partisan Media: The rise of partisan news outlets that cater to specific political ideologies has deepened divides by presenting biased perspectives.

Extremist Rhetoric: Political leaders and commentators using divisive language and promoting extreme viewpoints have fueled polarization.

Cultural and Social Issues:

Identity Politics: Debates over issues such as race, gender, and immigration have become highly charged and polarizing.

Economic Inequality: Growing economic disparities contribute to frustration and division among different social and economic groups.

Decline of Trust in Institutions:

Government and Media Distrust: Erosion of trust in traditional institutions, including the government and media, has led to increased skepticism and polarization.

Events Contributing to Polarization:

The 2016 Presidential Election:

Russian Interference: Reports of Russian interference in the 2016 election, including disinformation campaigns and social media manipulation, contributed to a highly polarized political environment.

FBI Investigation into Clinton's Emails: The FBI's handling of the investigation into Hillary Clinton's emails, including James Comey's public statements, intensified political divisions.

The 2020 Presidential Election and Capitol Riot:

Election Fraud Allegations: Unfounded claims of widespread voter fraud and election rigging led to deep political divisions and unrest.

Capitol Riot: The January 6, 2021, attack on the U.S. Capitol by supporters of Donald Trump was a manifestation of extreme polarization and highlighted the dangerous consequences of divisive rhetoric.

Black Lives Matter Protests and Responses:

Protests and Law Enforcement: The Black Lives Matter protests following incidents of police violence, such as the death of George Floyd, resulted in significant polarization around issues of race and policing.

Government Response: Responses to these protests, including controversial law enforcement tactics and rhetoric, further contributed to divisions.

COVID-19 Pandemic and Public Health Measures:

Mask Mandates and Vaccines: Disagreements over public health measures, such as mask mandates and vaccines, became highly polarizing issues, with debates often influenced by political and ideological divides.

Misinformation: The spread of misinformation about COVID-19, including its origins and treatment, exacerbated public confusion and polarization.

The Hunter Biden Laptop Controversy:

Media Coverage: The controversy surrounding Hunter Biden's laptop, and the alleged influence of foreign actors led to heated debates and polarized opinions about media bias and political corruption.

FBI and CIA Influences:

While there is no direct evidence that the FBI or CIA have intentionally manipulated events to increase polarization, their actions have sometimes contributed to a polarized environment:

FBI Surveillance and Investigations:

High-Profile Cases: Investigations into high-profile political figures and movements can contribute to polarized views, especially when controversial details are made public.

Leaks and Transparency: Leaks of sensitive information or selective disclosures can fuel partisan narratives and increase polarization.

CIA Operations and Disinformation:

Historical Disinformation Campaigns: The CIA's historical involvement in disinformation and covert operations, while not recent, has had long-term effects on public trust and political divisions.

Modern Influence: Although contemporary CIA operations are less overt, any involvement in shaping public perception or political outcomes can still influence polarization.

Polarization has worsened due to a complex interplay of technological, social, and political factors. While the FBI and CIA's actions have had various impacts, the primary drivers of polarization in recent years are more closely related to media dynamics, political rhetoric, and societal divisions. The focus on these issues highlights the need for better information literacy, responsible media practices, and efforts to bridge divides in an increasingly fragmented society.

Who benefits

In the context of increasing polarization and the influence of government agencies on public perception, several entities and groups can be seen as benefiting from the situation:

1. Political Leaders and Parties

Increased Influence: Politicians and political parties can benefit from heightened polarization by consolidating their base and increasing voter turnout among their supporters.

Control of Narrative: By leveraging the divisions within society, they can control the political narrative, rallying support for their policies and agendas.

2. Government Agencies

Expanded Authority: Agencies like the FBI and CIA may gain increased power and resources under the guise of national security and public order. This can lead to more surveillance, control, and influence over various social and political movements.

Justification for Actions: Increased polarization can justify more aggressive measures, including surveillance and interventions, as the government claims it is necessary for maintaining national security or public order.

3. Media Organizations

Higher Ratings and Revenue: Media outlets can benefit from polarized content by attracting more viewers or readers. Sensational and divisive news stories often lead to higher engagement and revenue through advertising and subscriptions.

Influence and Agenda Setting: Media organizations can shape public opinion and influence the political landscape by framing stories in ways that align with their interests or ideological leanings.

4. Special Interest Groups and Lobbyists

Increased Relevance: Polarization can amplify the voices of special interest groups and lobbyists who can leverage divisions to advance their agendas or secure funding and support.

Policy Influence: By capitalizing on existing divisions, these groups can push for policies that benefit their interests, often by framing issues in a way that resonates with polarized segments of the public.

5. Tech Companies and Social Media Platforms

User Engagement: Platforms like Facebook, Twitter, and others benefit from increased user engagement driven by divisive and sensational content. This can lead to greater data collection and advertising revenue.

Algorithmic Control: Tech companies can use algorithms to prioritize content that generates more engagement, often promoting divisive and controversial topics to keep users on their platforms longer.

6. Extremist and Radical Groups

Recruitment and Radicalization: Polarization can create an environment where extremist groups can more easily recruit and radicalize individuals by exploiting societal divisions and grievances.

Visibility and Influence: Increased media coverage and public attention to extreme viewpoints can give these groups more visibility and influence, allowing them to further their agendas.

7. Government Contractors and Security Firms

Increased Business: With heightened concerns about security and surveillance, private contractors and security firms that provide technology, training, and services to government agencies may see increased business opportunities.

8. Economic and Political Elites

Consolidation of Power: Economic and political elites can benefit from a divided and distracted populace, as it can prevent cohesive movements for systemic change that might threaten their interests.

Policy Advantages: Polarization can help these elites push through policies that favor their economic or political agendas while diverting public attention from critical issues.

In summary, the benefits of increased polarization and the manipulation of public perception extend to various actors in politics, media, technology, and beyond. Each group can leverage the divisions and disruptions for its gain, often at the expense of a more unified and equitable society.

Fighting back against COINTELPRO-like tactics and reversing some of the damage done requires not only a comprehensive strategy to protect against ongoing covert operations but also a focused effort to heal the communities and individuals affected by these tactics. COINTELPRO, the FBI's notorious counterintelligence program, sought to disrupt, discredit, and neutralize movements for civil rights, social justice, and political change. Today, similar tactics may still be in use, often under the guise of national security, making it imperative that we develop strategies to both resist these actions and repair the harm they have caused.

Public Awareness and Education

The first step in countering COINTELPRO-like activities is raising public awareness about the history and persistence of such tactics. This is the reason for this book. Education campaigns should focus on informing the public about the ways in which these methods have been used to undermine legitimate social movements and stifle dissent. This can be achieved through community workshops, educational programs in schools, public lectures, and widespread media coverage. Documentaries, books, and articles that detail the history and current implications of COINTELPRO-like operations can help the public understand the seriousness of these tactics. By making this knowledge accessible, communities can become more vigilant and better equipped to identify and counteract similar operations today.

Awareness should also extend to the specific communities and individuals historically targeted by COINTELPRO, such as civil rights leaders, activists, and minority groups. Special attention must be paid to educating these groups about the historical impact of COINTELPRO on their communities, helping them recognize patterns of state interference and manipulation that may still be present. This knowledge empowers them to resist ongoing efforts to undermine their work and rebuild their movements with greater resilience.

Legal Action and Advocacy

Legal action is a critical component in resisting COINTELPRO-like tactics and reversing the damage done. Citizens must advocate for stronger legal protections that prevent government agencies from engaging in illegal surveillance, infiltration, and disinformation campaigns. This involves pushing for legislation that clearly defines and prohibits such activities, with stringent penalties for those who violate the law. Independent oversight bodies should be established to monitor the activities of intelligence and law enforcement agencies, ensuring that they operate within the bounds of the law and respect civil liberties.

Litigation can also be a powerful tool for holding government agencies accountable. Victims of COINTELPRO-like tactics should be supported in seeking justice through the courts. Public interest law firms and civil rights organizations can play a vital role in this effort, offering legal representation and advocacy for those harmed by government overreach. Strategic litigation not only provides redress for victims but also sets legal precedents that can protect others from similar abuses in the future.

Reversing the damage done by COINTELPRO requires legal remedies as well. Efforts should be made to exonerate individuals who were wrongfully imprisoned or had their reputations destroyed as a result of COINTELPRO operations. Pardons, compensation, and public apologies are crucial steps in addressing the injustices of the past. Legal campaigns to clear the names of activists who were falsely accused or smeared can help restore their legacies and heal the communities they fought for.

Community Resilience and Healing

Building strong, resilient communities is essential in both resisting COINTELPRO-like tactics and repairing the damage they have caused. COINTELPRO often sought to divide and isolate individuals and groups, making them more vulnerable to state repression. To counter this, communities must foster solidarity and mutual support. Creating local networks that provide legal, emotional, and practical assistance to those targeted by state repression can help ensure that no one faces these challenges alone. These networks can also serve as platforms for collective action, allowing communities to respond quickly and effectively to new threats.

Healing the wounds inflicted by COINTELPRO requires more than just resistance; it also demands reconciliation and restoration. Communities must engage in processes of truth-telling and reconciliation, where the stories of those who were targeted can be heard and acknowledged. Public forums, truth commissions, and community-led inquiries can provide spaces for these stories to be shared, helping to bring closure and understanding. By addressing the trauma and division sown by COINTELPRO, communities can begin to heal and rebuild trust among their members.

Rebuilding the social movements that COINTELPRO sought to destroy is another critical aspect of reversing the damage. This can involve mentoring and training new generations of activists, ensuring that they are equipped with the knowledge and skills to execute the work of those who came before them. Supporting the revival of organizations that were weakened or dismantled by COINTELPRO, and helping them reconnect with their original missions, can restore their effectiveness and influence.

Technological Vigilance and Countermeasures

In today's digital age, technological vigilance is crucial in resisting COINTELPRO-like tactics. The rise of surveillance technologies and digital communication tools has made it easier for government agencies to monitor and disrupt activist movements. Educating citizens about digital security practices—such as using encryption, secure communication platforms, and privacy tools—can help protect personal information and prevent infiltration. Training in cybersecurity can safeguard against hacking, phishing, and other forms of digital sabotage.

Developing and promoting technological countermeasures is also important. Research into new methods for detecting and blocking illegal surveillance or disinformation campaigns can provide activists with the tools they need to defend themselves. Additionally, advocating for greater transparency and accountability in the development and use of surveillance technologies can help ensure that they are not misused against law-abiding citizens.

Transparency, Accountability, and Institutional Reform

Promoting transparency and accountability within government institutions is a key strategy in preventing COINTELPRO-like tactics from being used in the future. Citizens must advocate for reforms that increase oversight of intelligence and law enforcement agencies, ensuring that they operate within strict legal and ethical boundaries. This can include supporting legislation that limits the scope of covert operations, mandates regular audits of agency activities, and requires public reporting on their use of surveillance technologies.

Public pressure is also essential in demanding transparency from elected officials and holding them accountable for the actions of the agencies under their control. Campaigns that call for open government and the declassification of documents related to past and present covert operations can help expose abuses and prevent their recurrence. By shining a light on the activities of government agencies, citizens can create a culture of accountability that discourages illegal and unethical behavior.

Alliances with Media, Academia, and Human Rights Organizations

Forging alliances with media outlets, academics, and human rights organizations can amplify efforts to resist COINTELPRO-like tactics and reverse their effects. The media plays a crucial role in exposing government misconduct and informing the public about covert operations. Supporting investigative journalism that uncovers these activities can help bring them to light and create public pressure for change.

Academics can contribute valuable research that sheds light on the impact and mechanisms of state repression, providing evidence that can be used in legal and advocacy efforts. Collaborating with universities and research institutions to study the effects of COINTELPRO and similar programs can deepen our understanding of these tactics and inform strategies for resistance and healing.

Human rights organizations, both domestic and international, can apply pressure on governments to respect civil liberties and human rights. These organizations can advocate for victims, provide legal and financial support, and raise awareness on a global scale. By building a broad coalition that spans multiple sectors of society, citizens can create a powerful front against the misuse of government power.

Reversing the Damage

Reversing the damage done by COINTELPRO requires a long-term commitment to justice, healing, and reconciliation. This includes not only providing legal redress and public apologies for those who were wronged but also taking initiative-taking steps to rebuild the communities and movements that were targeted. Restoring the reputations of activists who were discredited, compensating those who suffered losses, and reviving organizations that were dismantled are all critical components of this effort.

In addition to these measures, fostering a national dialogue on the legacy of COINTELPRO and its impact on American society can help to heal the wounds it left behind. Recognizing and honoring the contributions of those who fought for civil rights and social justice, despite being targeted by COINTELPRO, can help restore their place in history and inspire future generations.

Combating COINTELPRO-like tactics and reversing the damage they have caused requires a multi-faceted approach that includes raising public awareness, legal action, community resilience, technological vigilance, transparency, and accountability. By addressing both the ongoing threat of these tactics and the harm they have already done, citizens can protect their rights, rebuild their communities, and ensure that the legacy of COINTELPRO is one of resistance and justice, rather than repression and fear.

About the Author

Tanya Tritchler is an exceptional researcher with a knack for uncovering the truth, no matter how well it's buried. As a proud military brat and a true patriot, Tanya loves her country fiercely but holds a healthy skepticism toward those in power. Fueled by curiosity and a bit of caffeine, she dives deep into the murky waters of government secrets, emerging with insights that will make you question everything. When she's not dissecting the latest political conundrum, you can find her enjoying the freedoms she holds dear—while keeping a wary eye on Big Brother.

www.ingramcontent.com/pod-product-compliance
Lightning Source LLC
Chambersburg PA
CBHW021425150726
47989CB00001B/121